MEETING GAME

T0078211

MEETING GAME

Make Meetings
EFFECTIVE, EFFICIENT AND ENERGETIC

MOHAN KARAMBELKAR
Foreword by Dr. David Lincoln

PARTRIDGE

A Penguin Random House Company

Copyright © 2013 by Mohan Karambelkar.

ISBN: Hardcover   978-1-4828-1225-1
           Softcover   978-1-4828-1224-4
           Ebook   978-1-4828-1223-7

All rights reserved. No part of this book may be used or reproduced by any means, graphic, electronic, or mechanical, including photocopying, recording, taping or by any information storage retrieval system without the written permission of the author and publisher except in the case of brief quotations embodied in critical articles and reviews.

Because of the dynamic nature of the Internet, any web addresses or links contained in this book may have changed since publication and may no longer be valid. The views expressed in this work are solely those of the author and do not necessarily reflect the views of the publisher, and the publisher hereby disclaims any responsibility for them.

To order additional copies of this book, contact
Partridge India
000 800 10062 62
www.partridgepublishing.com/india
orders.india@partridgepublishing.com

CONTENTS

i. Foreword

Mohan has taken the science and art of Neuro Linguistic Programming (NLP) to examine the delicate art of conducting a meeting. This is one of those things that a lot of us are involved in at some time in our life and yet are seldom, if ever, prepared for it.

Mohan has taken this area and examined it with his unique eye for detail. This book covers all aspects of conducting a meeting, from preparation to the tactics required, in all situations.

He has elegantly woven a lot of basic principles of NLP in a way that makes it easy for the reader to comprehend.

I highly recommend this book to all students of NLP and also managers and directors who find it necessary to conduct meetings of all types.

Armed with the details given in this book, you will become a master of meetings easily and effortlessly, be it a boardroom-level or just a quick meeting to discuss progress on sales or any other fields.

Dr David J. Lincoln Goa, May 2013
International NLP Master Trainer

ii. Preface

It was a business meeting of an airline company. The meeting facilitator was telling the meeting protocols. He said, 'Should there be a sudden loss of consciousness during the meeting, oxygen masks will drop from the ceiling.'

The same meeting was concluded by the chairperson of the meeting in this manner. 'OK. We spent hours and will make minutes. To conclude, I reiterate that we agree to go back to the cubicle and discuss why the solution discussed won't work.'

These jokes about meetings are commonly heard in offices, seen on Internet, or read in business articles. However, meetings are an important way of communication, yet they are ignored in terms of efficiency and effectiveness.

Meetings can be classified in several ways. On the basis of participants, there can be one-to-one meetings with two participants or a group meeting with several participants.

With globalisation and technology advances, meetings have become virtual meetings. People use audio conference or videoconference equipment. Another classification can be face-to-face meetings and virtual meetings.

Someone has classified meetings based on its frequency—regular meetings, ad hoc meetings, and emergency meetings. Another parameter could be duration of meeting. There can be a fifteen-minute stand-up meeting, one-to-two-hours staff meeting, or two-to-three-days conference.

Meetings can be classified as formal meetings and informal meetings. Informal meetings are conversions in informal setting. Formal meetings will have an agenda. This book focuses on formal meetings. Some of the concepts, for example, building rapport can be applicable to informal meetings as well.

During crises, meetings could be more for problem solving. During boom, meetings could be more for strategies and planning.

Whatever may be the purpose of the meeting or type of the meeting, meetings are the lifeblood of business communication. Efficiency and effectiveness of an organisation depend on how the meetings are conducted.

Efforts have been made to improve the meeting process. Robert's rule book has been available over a century and is useful for the administrative part of the meeting and for following a parliamentary procedure. Edward de Bono provided an excellent tool, Six Thinking Hats method, to boost efficiency and effectiveness. Another example could be Kepner and Tregoe's systematic approach to problem solving. This could be adopted for the meetings for problem solving.

Being a Toastmaster, I would like to mention how Toastmasters can help in your journey of improving communication and leadership skills, and it has a link to the meetings.

This book looks at meetings as a process and ponders how Neuro Linguistic Programming (NLP) can be used for meetings. NLP gels well with the conventional tools or techniques and gives further boost to effectiveness, efficiency, and energy. NLP is enriched with tips on rapport building, outcome definition, language usage, communication, and many more things that will make meetings effective, efficient, and energetic. This book uses simple language so that persons without NLP knowledge can also grasp NLP concept.

If you are more curious about NLP, then the best thing is to attend NLP course. NLP training levels are NLP practitioner, NLP master practitioner, NLP train the trainer, and master trainer of NLP. I have referred to almost all the levels while writing this book and did not put any restriction. As International NLP Master Trainer Dr David Lincoln says, 'If you start with practitioner level, you will develop interest in NLP and you will go on doing higher levels to become NLP trainer.'

If you are already an NLP practitioner, this book will provide insight into efficiency and effectiveness for your business through better meetings.

When people are motivated, they treat and enjoy work as play. On similar lines, we can consider a meeting as a sport event; we can derive analogy with sport.

For successful meetings, it requires an effectiveness of an archer to aim at a good decision, efficiency of a sprinter to achieve maximum out of time, and energy of a weightlifter to lift action items to the level of achievement.

NLP is used in sports for improving the performance of sportspersons. This book explores the use of NLP for conducting meetings. It gives a reason for executives and businesspersons to use NLP in daily life, especially for meetings.

Being an NLP practitioner, I have avoided negative language or focus on negative terms like *bad meetings*, *sins of meetings*, *deadly meeting*, *meeting monster*, and many other negative terms. If we talk about negative terms, it will attract the same. We wish to move towards good meetings; hence, we focus on concepts, tools, and techniques for good meetings.

iii. Acknowledgement

Being a quality assurance professional, I have focused on implementing quality standards and quality frameworks in various organisations. For leadership and communication skills, I joined Toastmasters in 2005 in Singapore and later started clubs in Pune (India). At Toastmasters Club, Mr Ganesh Srinivasan introduced me to NLP, and then my association with NLP and HUNA group, Pune, started. I would like to thank Mr Ganesh Srinivasan.

I studied NLP courses at ANLP, Goa. I am fully indebted to trainers Dr David Lincoln, Mr Ralph Watson, Sushil Mehrotra, and Umesh Soman.

I appreciate Dr David Lincoln for giving in-depth knowledge on NLP in lucid manner and Mr Ralph Watson for giving business perspective of NLP. Their training and guidance encouraged me to bring out this book.

I would like to thank NLP and HUNA group, especially Ganesh Srinivasan, Vikas Dikshit, Gaikwad, and Prof Apte for their knowledge sharing.

I also thank Toastmasters clubs, especially ACCA Toastmasters, Singapore, Toastmasters Club of Pune, and Eaton Toastmasters Club for all the learning about meetings and for the feedback from DTM Vincent Lim, DTM Prasad Sovani, TM April Tan, TM Manish Kulkarni, TM Mandar Bapat, and many other Toastmasters.

I would like to thank Mr Manas Karambelkar for creatively adding pictures for this book. I would like to thank Mrs Supriya Karambelkar for checking this book for grammar, with a reader's perspective.

I would like to thank Partridge team for giving final shape to this book.

Mohan Karambelkar

iv. About the Author

Mohan Karambelkar has a unique combination of qualifications—being an engineer from IIT Mumbai (M Tech in Reliability Engineering) and an accountant (qualified from ACCA UK and CIMA UK). He also has certifications like CISA from ISACA (USA), CSQA from QAI (USA), and ITIL Expert from EXIN (Netherland). His twenty-four years of experience includes mainly quality management and software development. He has worked with IT department, engineering department, and accounting department. He is associated with ANLP India and is a certified NLP trainer. He is a member of Toastmasters since September 2005 and has achieved the highest title, 'Distinguished Toastmaster'. He also owns the Pune-based PQR Consultancy Services LLP, the firm that provides consultancy for productivity, quality, and reliability.

MEETING GAME

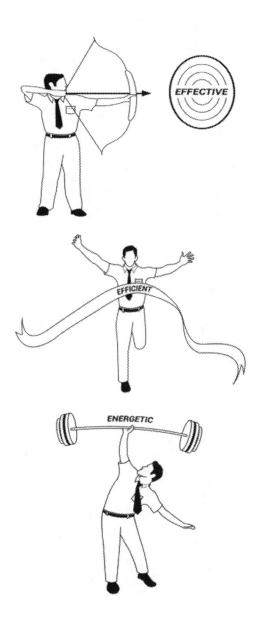

1. Introduction

The dictionary meaning of *meeting* is 'an act of coming together' or 'an assembly or conference for a common purpose'. However, when we talk about meetings, many executives feel conducting meetings is waste of time and often question how to survive in the long-winded aimless meeting. Over the years, the meeting has acquired a bad reputation among the executives. However, meetings provide an excellent opportunity to exercise communication skills, leadership skills, and thinking skills. Any organisation, small or large, uses meetings for its operation. Instead of looking at meetings as a necessary evil, it is better to look at it as a tool for effective and efficient operation.

1.1　Factors for Successful Meeting

Surveys and brainstorming sessions have been conducted to find the cause of effective/ineffective meetings. These surveys and sessions have come up with several factors. I would like to apply 80:20 rule (20 per cent factors causing 80 per cent impact) and come up with three major factors.

Top three factors (3Ps) for successful meetings are the following:

1. Purpose—Meetings must have a clear purpose. Different purposes of meetings could be the following:
    a. Planning meetings like deciding the strategies and plans
    b. Status meetings like monthly meetings or staff meetings to inform the status
    c. Decision meetings like brainstorming followed by problem solution

    Formal meetings can fall under one of these meetings or combination of these meetings. Purpose of a meeting is discussed in depth in Chapter 2.

2. Programme (or agenda)—The purpose is to be elaborated through a programme or an agenda. The meeting should be planned with adequate time to address each item on the programme or agenda. It is ensured that all items in the programme or agenda are addressed. This has been addressed in Chapter 4.

3. Participation—Participation is vital for the meeting's success. We should invite the people who have a clear role in the meeting proceedings and schedule the meeting in such a way that the participants can study the related issues and can come well prepared for the meeting. We should encourage participation during the meeting. This has been addressed in Chapter 5.

Top three factors (3Ds) for unsuccessful meetings are the following:

1. Drift from the subject—Intentional or unintentional diversion to other topics will defeat the purpose of the meeting. This is a challenge for the facilitator to handle the people. This is discussed in Chapter 3.

2. Deficient preparation—Lack of preparation by the participants will result in lack of quality discussion during the meeting and may result in poor decision-making. This has been addressed in Chapter 4.

3. Deferral for actions—When a meeting does not come to consensus, it fails to conclude, and no decisions are made or follow-up actions are deferred. This has been addressed in Chapter 6.

Our objective is to bring in the factors of success and to push out the factors of unsuccessful meetings and make meetings effective, efficient, and energetic. This needs support of system, strategy, and synergy.

Top three things (3Es) to be achieved for meetings are the following:

1. Efficiency—Efficiency means doing things right. This is about productivity. In case of a meeting, it is optimised use of resources. In a running race, an athlete wishes to cover the distance in minimum time. The productivity or efficiency indicates the ratio of output (distance) to input (time). As time (of executive) is a

major resource, shorter meetings will give higher efficiency. This does not mean it should be at the cost of effectiveness.

2. Effectiveness—Effectiveness means doing right things. In case of a meeting, it is the extent to which the purpose of the meeting is served or achieved. This is about the quality—quality of discussion and quality of decision. In case of archery, an archer does not focus on how fast he or she shoots; the archer focuses on how accurate he or she is on his or her target. In a meeting, today's decisions become tomorrow's reality. Accuracy or correctness of decision in a meeting is important.

3. Energy—Sound meeting practices will not drain the energy of the participants. Positive results from the meeting will boost the energy, and participants are highly motivated to take action items. This is about the reliability that quality decisions are transformed into quality actions that finally achieve desired results. In case of weightlifting, weightlifter exerts force or builds energy to lift the weights. In case of meetings, meetings should provide energy to finish tasks successfully. Realities will happen when tasks are completed.

Top three things (3S) to be provided for a meeting are the following:

1. System—This consists of structure, process, guidelines, tools, techniques, and so on provided for the success of a meeting. A meeting is viewed as a transformation process from a concept to an implemented action. System adopts the good practices.

2. Strategy—This sets the direction for achieving purpose. These are not rigid rules. These are plans with flexibility. Formal meetings need strategic thinking in sequencing the items on agenda. If six thinking hats method is used for the meeting, blue hat thinking (that is, thinking about thinking) will give the strategy for using other thinking hats.

3. Synergy—This is a people factor or a required mind set for the meetings. The mindset is 'together everyone achieves more', and the participants have a win-win approach. Every executive has strengths and weaknesses. When the executives participate in a meeting, they complement each other with their strengths and produce better results with synergy.

Meetings not producing desired results or outcomes are generally due to lack of process, ignorance on people factors, and not using tool and techniques. First, we will look at meetings as a process. The people factors are seen in Chapter 3. The tools and techniques are seen in all chapters.

Each chapter provides NLP concepts as well as some of the conventional recommendations. NLP concepts are simple yet influential techniques for the meetings.

1.2   Meeting Process

Process can be defined in different ways. We can visualise the process flow by looking at swimlane diagram. High-level swimlane diagram is shown in Figure 1.1.

Detailed process can be defined in terms of hierarchy, input, process, and output (see Figure 1.2). All inputs and outputs can be assessed for the entry criteria and exit criteria, respectively. The inputs/outputs (intermediate and final) for the meetings are purpose, agenda, preparation, decision, and actions. For the best result, quality of these should be high.

Another way to look at process is RACI chart (see Figure 1.3). RACI stands for *responsible, accountable, consulted,* and *informed.* This provides clarity on the roles in the process and clarity on responsibilities and accountability.

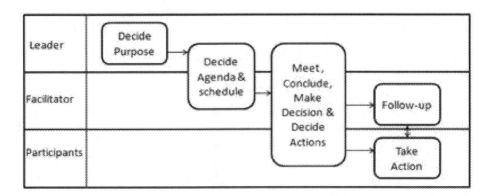

Figure 1.1: Swimlane diagram.

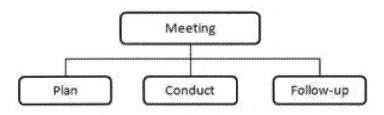

Input	Process	Output
Plan		
Plan initiative - Purpose or expected outcome	Detail plan for a meeting - Check the participants required - Check the resources availability - Expand the purpose into an agenda	Meeting Plan - Agenda - Schedule (time, duration, venue) - Assigned roles - Accepted meeting request
Conduct		
Meeting inputs - Agenda - Participants and their preparation - Resources – room and equipments	Conduct a meeting - Participate in discussion - Decision making - Recording	Meeting output - Decision - Follow-up action
Follow-up		
Meeting output - Action item	Report progress and complete action	Desired outcome

Figure 1.2: Hierarchy Input–process–output chart for a meeting.

Activities	Leader	Facilitator	Participant(s)	Admin	Recorder/Timer
Decide the purpose/ need for a meeting	R				
Plan the meeting/agenda	A	R			
Book the resources and block participants' calendar for the meeting	C	C	I	R	I
Distribute agenda/ information required for the meeting	A	R			
Prepare for the meeting	R	R	R		
Opening the meeting	R	R			
Discussion	A/R	R	R		
Track Time through-out meeting					R
Record notes of the meeting					R
Closing the meeting; Feedback	A	R			
Follow-up action	A	R	R		

Figure 1.3: RACI chart for a meeting.

Roles defined in the RACI chart are generic. One person may perform multiple roles. Roles may be as per the meeting speciality. In case of a process review meeting, the participants can be producers (who have defined the process) and reviewers (who provide a feedback). Some meetings will have the role of a parliamentarian who assures that Robert rule book is followed. Some organisations use different terms; presiding officer or chairperson will be a facilitator, and secretary may be a recorder.

1.3   Process Maturity

Another aspect of a process is its maturity level. Quality Guru Philip Crosby suggested quality management maturity grid. Software companies used this concept for process improvement based on CMMI framework. This can be applied to meetings.

Level 1 process (initial) is chaotic. The success of a meeting depends on heroics of an individual. There is a lack of standard practices in an organisation, and there is no control. This can often result in blames and accusation. The system, strategy, and synergy (3Ss) will be missing. The efficiency, effectiveness, and energy (3Es) are not at all expected.

Level 2 process (repeatable) has some credibility. The meetings are conducted in a consistent manner to some extent. However, there are no process documents or training for process. Still there is a high reliance on the individuals. The system for the meetings exists with ambiguity; however, strategy and synergy are missing. The efficiency, effectiveness, and energy (3 E) are not significant.

Level 3 process (defined) is standardised and documented. Tools and techniques are recommended in the process, and the process training helps to implement consistency across the organisation. Meetings will have a well-defined system with tools and techniques. There will be significant improvement in efficiency and effectiveness. Strategy for a meeting may appear. However, people factor (synergy) may still be missing. There is no monitoring or measurements. Hence, achievement of efficiency and effectiveness is not reported.

Level 4 process (managed and measured or quantitatively managed) is a process where performance indicators are monitored. The evidence procedure is well defined, process is measured, and controls are improved. The systems are further improved for monitoring. What gets measured gets managed. Strategy will be used for better results. Executives will be aware of the importance of synergy. There is achievement of efficiency and effectiveness.

Level 5 process (optimised) is a process with system, strategy, and synergy (3S). Process will have continual improvements. Process (meeting) will have creativity, innovation, and high motivation. This will have effectiveness, efficiency, and energy (3E). NLP techniques can play important role in achieving this process level.

Figure 1.4 shows the system, strategy, and synergy (3S) as inputs and efficiency, effectiveness, and energy (3E) as outputs at each process maturity level.

Process Maturity	System	Strategy	Synergy	Efficiency	Effectiveness	Energy
	Inputs			Outputs		
Level 1 (Initial)	○	○	○	○	○	○
Level 2 (Repeatable)	◐	○	○	○	○	○
Level 3 (Defined)	●	◐	○	◐	◐	○
Level 4 (Quantitatively Managed)	●	◐	◐	●	●	◐
Level 5 (Optimized)	●	●	●	●	●	●

○ Absence　　　◐ Partial Presence　　　● Presence

Figure 1.4: 3S and 3E for process maturity levels.

1.4　In Summary

Organisations often assume that executives will learn about the meetings automatically through experience, or it is considered as 'on the job training'. Though it looks like common sense, common sense is not so common. Organisations often find dos and don'ts about the meetings. However, it is difficult to implement the improvements by listing the dos and don'ts.

Process approach can be adopted for the meetings. This will bring the best practices, use of tools and techniques, and importance of continual improvement. Highest process maturity (level 5) will have system, strategy, and synergy (3S) in place and will achieve efficiency, effectiveness, and energy (3E).

1.5 Afterthought

After going through this chapter, you will have thoughts about the discussion in this chapter. Our theme is to build the systems, strategies and synergies for the meetings. With due respect to your model of the world, please jot down your thoughts on systems, strategies and synergies

- What are the systems needed for a meeting?

_____

_____

_____

- What are the strategies required for a meeting?

_____

_____

_____

- How are synergies built for a meeting?

_____

_____

_____

MEETING GAME WITH PURPOSE

2. Do I Need a Meeting?

Ken Blanchard said, 'None of us is as smart as all of us.' When we need to exchange ideas to make a smart decision with consensus among all, meetings will be the best option. As businesses cannot be run in isolation, interactions and meetings are very much a part of it. This chapter focuses on the need of a meeting or the purpose of a meeting.

The biggest sporting event on earth is Olympics. The high-level purpose of promoting Olympics is to promote ethics and fair play in sport. Sports create fun as well as encourage sportsman spirit. Similarly, meetings should have high-level purpose. Meetings should serve a clear purpose and should give fun and energy to the meeting participants. This chapter provides a tool for defining purpose and its assessment.

2.1 Meetings and Other Options

When an executive decides to have a meeting, he or she should assess the alternative communication options like an email or a phone call. Every communication has limitations; hence, it is a careful selection of right option to optimise the efforts on effectiveness and efficiency.

The possible question can be—can this be handled by a phone call or a discussion is required? If more than one person is needed for the discussion, a meeting will be the better option.

Email is a quicker and cheaper communication tool with global reach. We can send an email to multiple recipients. However, a long report like emails or email chains with multiple comments are difficult to digest. Time will be wasted in understanding the different views from the email chain. In such a situation, a meeting will be the better option.

When an executive wish to get a feedback on proposal or wish to reconcile the differences (different opinions) and reach consensus, a meeting is the better option.

As an executive moves to higher ranks in an organisation, he or she needs to deal with more people, and meetings may increase exponentially. Senior executives should realise the importance of effectiveness and efficiency in conducting meetings.

The requirement of a meeting can be assessed by looking at its purpose. The purpose of the meeting will consider the goals or outcomes to be achieved from the meeting. Another important aspect is the cost associated with the meeting. Decision of having meeting should be cost-effective. Hence, this chapter highlights the meeting cost. Then we can apply NLP to bring clarity to the purpose.

Before looking into the cost and NLP techniques, it is good to look at the types of meetings. Each type of meetings will serve different purposes.

2.2   Types of Meetings

Meetings can have several classifications based on the following:

- participants (one-to-one, one-to-many, group, or team meetings),
- frequency (routine or regular meetings, ad hoc meetings, or emergency meetings), and
- physical presence (face-to-face meetings or virtual meetings).

Roles in an organisation will call for different types of meetings. Sales persons may have meetings with customers. It could be a cold call, a persuasive proposal, or a winning deal. On the other side, buyer organisation may call for meetings for their request for proposal (RFP).

Project teams will have meetings for a project, which may include project kick-off meetings, project progress meetings, meetings for project milestones/project phase, and project hand-over/closing meetings, and so on.

Operations team may have stand-up meetings of short duration for status check.

Quality management group may have brainstorming session meetings for generating ideas for improvements, meetings for problem solving, and meetings for review or assessment.

Technology group will have technical presentation meetings or new product proposal. Marketing group will have market strategy meetings, product strategy meetings, and so on.

Management will have meetings for decision-making, policy setting, and so on.

Boards will have meetings for policy/direction setting, result reporting, and so on.

Administrative meetings will include meetings like staff meetings, department meetings, and so on.

If meetings are legal requirement (for example conducting annual general meeting—AGM), they are to be as per those legal requirements.

This list is not exhaustive. As each organisation has its own terminology for the meetings, each organisation can have its own comprehensive list of meetings.

To have a simple classification, we can have the following three types:

1. *Meetings for strategies and planning*—These are forward-looking meetings, exploring opportunities. This will focus on transformation or desired change
2. *Meetings for problem solving*—These could be pressing problems which are important and urgent. The other could be problem prevention. These are also forward-looking. These focus on restoring normalcy or maintaining normalcy.
3. *Meetings for status reporting*—These are for feedback or a monitoring mechanism. These could be routine or regular meetings, focusing on transactions. It is good to keep regular meetings to minimum.

Stephen Covey's third habit, 'put first thing first', is applicable to meetings. Meetings can be seen in time-management matrix with two parameters—urgency and importance. Important but not urgent meetings will focus on future, vision, mission, and so on and problem prevention. It is good to have these meetings. Important and urgent meetings are required for crises. It will be good to have minimum crises and minimum meetings for crises. Not important but urgent meetings are planning failures and have lack of control. Not important and not urgent meetings are waste of time or keeping busy with trivial things.

2.3   Meeting Cost

Another important aspect is meeting cost. Meeting cost will include labour cost, that is, hourly cost of each participant. When the participants are holding higher posts in the organisation, the hourly cost to the company will be higher.

There will be a cost of venue. Meetings use facilities like a conference room or a meeting room. It has the overhead cost. In addition, meetings may require equipment for audio conference or videoconference and related services. These are overheads or direct service cost. If an offsite venue is used, cost will be higher.

Some executives travel distances across a country or across the globe for meetings. There is a huge travel cost as a part of meetings.

An executive should look for an opportunity cost. If the meeting time would have been spent on other activity, the benefits could be achieved through that activity. Those benefits are the opportunity cost.

An executive need not become a cost accountant to calculate accurate gains and expenses of the meetings. However, an executive should be aware that meetings make optimal use of resources.

In case of urgent meeting, we need to resolve the crises; continuation of crises can lead to more losses and thus, meetings prevent the further loss. The not urgent and not important meetings will be a huge loss because there is no value addition activity. The important but not urgent meetings will have value addition activities.

2.4   Purpose of Meeting

Toastmasters' communication manual defines the purpose of delivering a speech in two levels—a general purpose and a specific purpose. The general purpose can be to inform, to persuade, to entertain, or to inspire. The specific purpose is one statement you wish to accomplish. This concept can be extended to meetings.

Meetings to inform are meetings for knowledge transfer, technical demonstration, process briefing, and so on. These meetings should be interactive to make them interesting.

Meetings to persuade are sales meetings. Most of the meetings will fall under this category because we sell our ideas, our products, or our services.

Formal meetings cannot be for entertainment. However, humour has importance in the meeting. Humour will be discussed in Chapter 9.

A leader needs to motivate others and inspire them to take challenges. He or she should look at meetings as an opportunity to motivate.

The specific purpose is to make one-sentence statement about what you wish to accomplish in the meeting. It is the foundational phrase upon which the meeting is based.

If 'six thinking hats' methodology is used in the organisation, blue hat thinking is handy for defining the purpose. One of the key aspects is to determine the focus of the meeting. The broad focus can be exploratory (brainstorming) or specific (problem solving). The questions under blue hat thinking can derive the specific purpose. The facilitator (wearing blue thinking hat) can control the deviations during the meeting by considering the purpose.

If purpose is not clearly stated, the discussion will be diverse and disjointed. It will be difficult for the participants to do adequate preparation. For example, once an IT manager sent a meeting request with vaguely defined purpose: 'We will meet for PMC.' A newly joined IT analyst thought PMC means project management controls and prepared accordingly. At the meeting, he came to know that PMC stands for production migration control (that is, transferring computer programs from test environment to production/live environment). There may be many questions on the topic: is the meeting meant for discussing the tool for production migration? Are there issues or incidents because of incorrect transfer of computer programs? Are there security concerns and access control issues? Finally, the IT manager started the discussion about releases (production migration) planned for next month. Without clear purpose and adequate information, participants cannot prepare and the leader will not achieve the desired outcome.

If the purpose of a regular meeting is just to have a meeting, then the meeting becomes fruitless. Hence, it is good to have minimum regular meetings.

2.5 NLP Perspective for Purpose

NLP can be useful to define and assess the specific purpose. The leader (executive) must be clear about the purpose of a meeting or outcome expected from the meeting. The NLP-based checks are useful for defining the purpose as well as assessment.

2.5.1 Is It Stated in a Positive Manner?

As per NLP, positive statements will have better success than negative statements. Unconscious mind does not process the negatives. When we say, 'Do not make errors', unconscious mind thinks about errors and may result in more errors. Meetings should have their objective in a positive manner.

If the meeting objective is to reduce the rejection rate in the manufacturing unit, the positive statement could be to improve the acceptance rate. If the meeting objective is to overcome a problem of over-capacity in dwindling economy, the positive statement could be to optimise the plant capacity for cost-effectiveness.

Edward de Bono mentioned in his books on thinking that western organisations usually treat improvements as getting rid of faults, defects, bottlenecks, high-cost areas, complaint areas, and problems. This is dangerous because when you fix the problem, you are back at where you were before you had the problem. Thus, you miss the real improvement. Thus, positive statements will have wider implication on improvement.

Stephen Covey's first habit, 'Be proactive', also suggests the use of proactive language, which is very positive. Meetings will be successful (effective, efficient, and energetic) if the leader's approach is positive.

Another important concept in NLP is perception filter—'away and towards'. 'Away from' people will look from avoidance perspective. 'Towards' people are motivated and look from achievement perspective.

A leader with 'away' perception will say, 'I am conducting one-to-one meetings with my subordinates as management monitors the number of one-to-one meetings, and I wish to avoid any non-compliance.'

A leader with 'towards' perception will say, 'One-to-one meetings with my subordinate is an excellent opportunity to coach them and subsequently achieve team goals.'

A leader with 'away' perception will say, 'It is boring, but I do not want to break the routine briefing of financial number.'

A leader with 'towards' perception will say, 'We will look at the financial figures and hone our skills of interpreting financial data and get understanding of financial facts.'

A 'towards' leader will state the purpose in a positive manner.

2.5.2 Is the Check on Ecology Done?

This check is to assess the gains and losses and also the consequences in different situations. These are shown in Figure 2.1.

What would happen if you conduct a meeting (achieve the outcome)? This clearly looks at the gains.

What would not happen if you conduct a meeting (achieve the outcome)? This looks at the loss of current gains or current benefits.

What would happen if you didn't conduct a meeting (did not achieve the outcome)? This will look at the cost of continuing with current status or having status quo.

What would not happen if you didn't conduct a meeting (did not achieve the outcome)? This is a difficult question. Logically, you may think of not making gains. It is best to answer the question intuitively rather than logically.

The example of Cartesian coordinate is in Figure 2.2.

Converse	Theorem
~AB	**AB**
Example	Example
What would not happen if you did ___ ?	What would happen if you did ___ ?
Non-mirror Image Reverse	Inverse
~A~B	**A~B**
Example	Example
What would not happen if you did not ___ ?	What would happen if you did not ___ ?

Figure 2.1: Cartesian coordinate.

Converse What would not happen if you did?	*Theorem* - What would happen if you did?
• IT analysts are happy to work on simple IT requests. It is in their comfort zone. • IT users are happy with the quick response of IT department. This leads to good customer satisfaction scores.	• Substantial IT request will be faster and with no IT analyst's intervention. This will reduce IT operation cost. • IT projects will not have a constraint of IT analyst busy with IT operations. • IT analyst will have more challenging work.
Non-mirror Image Reverse What would not happen if you did not? • Cost reduction would not happen as per expectations. Outsourcing can be considered for cost reduction.	*Inverse* What would happen if you did not? • With the growth of an organisation, the simple request will increase. This may need more IT analysts and this will result in high IT staff cost • With focus on IT operation, IT projects will be delayed and will not be taken up.

Figure 2.2: Example of ecology check using Cartesian coordinate.

For example, a chief information officer (CIO) asks to call a meeting to find the means of reducing the volume of simple requests to IT department. He or she is concerned about the large amount of time spent by IT analysts on serving the simple requests. His or her expectations are to automate or develop a self-help so that IT analysts will be available for activities with higher value addition. The expected meeting should brainstorm to find the ways of reducing the number of simple IT requests and implement the best option. The purpose of the meeting can be analysed through ecology checks.

2.5.3 Is the Neurological Level Checked?

Meetings are change catalysts. Change may be major or minor. Meetings are used for every stage of change—need for change, design, implementation, and post-implementation. The purpose of the meeting can be assessed on the change that will take place through the meeting. This will give an idea on the level of thinking required. NLP concept called neurological level (Figure 2.3 and Table 2.1) is useful in assessing the change. Robert Dilts developed this idea based on the concept formulated by anthropologist Gregory Bateson.

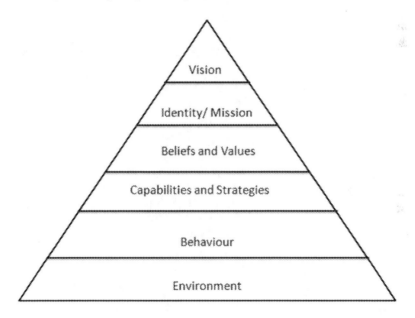

Figure 2.3 Neurological levels.

A leader or an executive can have better understanding of the purpose of the meeting by looking at the following questions:

- At what level, do we need a discussion in the meeting? The higher level will have impact on all lower levels.

Level	Questions or details to look for
1. Purpose/ Vision	What is the most important thing an organisation wants to do (for the next five, ten, or twenty years)? It is a conceptual and purposeful foresight. What do we expect from an organisation (customers to be served and your connection to a larger system – community, country, or world)?
2. Identity/ Mission	Who are you as an organisation? What role does an organisation play to achieve its purpose or vision? This is an internally focused statement, setting direction and governance.
3. Beliefs and values	What factors are important for an organisation for working situations? These are like compass that guides the decisions and makes out what is right and what is wrong. This gives the work ethics.
4. Capabilities/ Strategies	What skills, competencies, and knowledge does an organisation have? What are the long-term plans, medium-term plans, and short-term plans? This will provide processes at which organisation is best or wants to be the best
5. Behaviour	What are the behaviours of the staff while working in an organisation? Is it distressful or fun? Is it energetic or tiring? This will give a motivation level.
6. Environment	Where, when, and with whom a person needs to work? What are the external influences? This will provide processes, procedures, and interaction with internal and external groups.

Table 2.1: Neurological levels' details

– Albert Einstein said, 'The problems of today can only be solved at a higher level of thinking than that at which created them.' This gives an idea on how to look at the problem and the required level of thinking.

– How do you see alignment at different levels? Change should not result in misalignment.

Another important aspect is organisation level at which each neurological level is dealt with. Junior-level executives will be dealing with environment level (level 6); middle-level executives may be dealing with levels 4 and 5, that is, capabilities and behaviour; and senior executives focus at levels 1, 2, and 3, that is, vision, mission, and values.

2.5.4 Is Evidence Procedure Checked?

This is to check how you will know that the meeting has achieved its purpose. The meeting will result in actionable items. If no actionable items are expected, then the purpose of the meeting is ambiguous. Evidence procedure is discussed in detail for action items in Chapter 6.

2.6   In Summary

Many executives schedule regular meetings with little thought on the purpose. Various items with little or no connection with purpose will be included in the agenda and the meeting will lack direction. To set a clear direction, decide the general purpose of the meeting—to persuade, to inspire, or to inform. Skilfully used humour (to entertain) can add value to the meeting. The specific purpose will be based on the functional aspects and a foundation statement. It is also a foundation for strategy and synergy. NLP techniques are useful for clarity in defining purpose and its assessment. The purpose should be a positive statement and should be assessed for ecology and level of discussion. When you have a clear purpose for the meeting, you definitely need a meeting.

As a part of a system, we looked at the tools like meeting costing, Cartesian coordinate, neurological levels, and concept of expressing in positive manner.

Our strategy is to evaluate the purpose of a meeting thoroughly, using tools, and ensure that the purpose is stated in a positive manner.

2.7 Afterthought

After going through this chapter, you will have thoughts about the discussion in this chapter. Our theme is to build the systems, strategies and synergies for the meetings. With due respect to your model of the world, please jot down your thoughts on systems, strategies and synergies.

- What are the systems needed for a meeting?

_____

_____

_____

- What are the strategies required for a meeting?

_____

_____

_____

- How are the synergies built for a meeting?

_____

_____

_____

KNOW THE PLAYERS
OF THE MEETING GAME

3. Who Are the Participants in a Meeting?

Participants are the key to the success of a meeting. Facilitator faces the challenge to get the maximum out of the participants. At organisational level, human resources department takes care of people factor. At meeting level, the facilitator needs to take care of people factor and group dynamics. The leader will have a question. 'Whom do I invite for the meeting?' This needs an analysis for the required participation, and the leader needs to think on how he or she should understand different people. If we know the people well, we can build a rapport and utilise their talent and get the best outcome.

Team games like soccer, hockey, or cricket require talents of different types. Soccer and hockey need forward, midfielder, defenders, and goalkeeper. In case of cricket, it is batsman, bowler, fielders, and wicketkeeper. Players will have their own style, strengths, and weaknesses. When players know each other well, build cooperation, and develop synergy, the team will experience success. In case of a meeting (an organisation), there is a need for different talent and synergy among them so that meetings, and ultimately organisation, will be successful.

This chapter gives a process perspective (RACI chart), behaviour perspective (conventional concept, MBTI), motivation perspective, communication perspective (representational system), group perspective (group dynamics), and global perspective. NLP presuppositions are discussed in some of the sections so that we can have a positive approach towards various aspects and situations.

3.1 Process Perspective

When we decide the purpose or have a tentative meeting agenda, we also look at the persons to be invited for the meeting. One useful tool is RACI chart (responsible, accountable, consulted, and informed). Example of RACI chart is in Figure 1.3. Persons shown 'responsible' in RACI chart must be invited as they will be responsible for the actions.

This group drives the implementation. Accountable persons are the senior persons or senior management. We need to keep them in a loop, and also their approvals are sought. We should make a decision to invite them based on the importance of agenda item(s) and their availability. Senior management may delegate their authority and empower subordinates to make the decisions. People to be consulted can be optional participants, depending on their value addition. People under 'consulted' category may be subject matter experts. Need of their expertise should be assessed. People to be informed need to be assessed in terms of impact so that their presence in the meeting is decided. Ensure that important stakeholders are covered. When an executive is not sure, it is good to consult other people and finalise the participants.

We have also seen neurological-level assessment and set expected level of discussion. It is good to explore who are responsible for the specific level. Vision, mission, strategies, and long-term plans are dealt by senior management, and they have a perspective of the whole organisation. Capabilities, strategies, behaviour, and medium-term plans are dealt by middle management, and they have perspective of their department or cross-functional activities. Lowest 'environment' level is dealt by junior management, and they have an operational perspective. Appropriate level of executives should be considered based on the meeting purpose.

Some people are title-sensitive, for example, if there is a meeting between an accounts department and IT department and the account department's head is attending that meeting, then he or she may expect the IT department's head to attend the meeting.

We need to consider people for meeting roles like facilitator or secretary. We need to decide whether the participants can take these roles or we need to invite someone for the meeting roles. If a meeting is using six thinking hats, it is good to have a facilitator who is certified on De Bono thinking system. Kepner Tregoe model also has a certification for process facilitator and coach.

In short, we need to ensure that all the participants have a reason for attending the meeting.

3.2 Participants' Classification

Studies (non-NLP) have classified different participants into different groups (refer Table 3.1, 3.2, 3.3, 3.4 and 3.5). This classification is based on three papers. First paper is by H. C. Wedgewood, 'Fewer Camels, More Horses: Where Committees Go Wrong', *Personnel*, Vol. 44, No. 4, July-August 1967, pp. 62-87. (This is also quoted in Pearce, Figgins, and Golen, *Principles of Business Communication: Theory, Application, and Technology*. New York: John Wiley & Sons, 1984, pp. 383-384.) Second paper is by Sadler and Tucker, *Common Ground: A Course in Communication*. South Melbourne: Macmillan, 1981, p. 82. Third paper is Kathy Takamaya, Brown University, *Facilitating Group Discussion: Understanding group development and dynamics,* Essay on Teaching Excellence: Towards the best in the academy, Volume 21, Number 1, 2009-10

Many presentations on meetings have referred to these papers. However, we are analysing the classification with NLP concepts.

These classifications may label participants and put them into categories supportive or disruptive. There are suggestions to handle disruptive members. For example, ask silent participants for their comments or opinion. In case of a dominant member, redirect the question to other members.

Labelling a person is not a right thing. This will develop prejudices about the labelled person, and the labelled person may have a negative belief in him or her.

If 'six thinking hats' method is used for a meeting, Edward de Bono suggests that the participants should not be labelled by the hats. Every participant has an ability to think differently by adopting different hats. Six thinking hats is a methodology for thinking and not for labelling.

Role	Behaviour	Details
Group Building role	The initiator	Brings in new/different ideas
	The opinion giver	States pertinent beliefs about the discussion or others' suggestions
	The elaborator	Constructs on suggestions made by others
	The rationalist	Makes worthwhile contributions, ideas are well thought-out

Table 3.1: Constructive behaviour in a meeting (Participants' classifications)

Role	Behaviour	Details
Maintenance Role (Supportive)	The tension reliever	Uses humour or calls for a break at the appropriate moments
	The compromiser	Willing to give up when necessary for progress
	The clarifier	Offers rationales, probes for meaning, restates the problems
	The tester	Raises the questions to test if the group is ready to come to a decision
	The summariser	Pulls the discussion together, reviews the progress so far.
	The harmoniser	Mediates the differences of opinion, reconciles the points of view
	The encourager	Praises and supports others in their contributions
	The gate keeper	Keeps the communications open, creates the opportunities for participation
	The process checker	Checks the compliance to the process and procedures and alerts the participants
	The know-all	Tries to monopolize, but can have good ideas.

Table 3.2: Supportive behaviour in a meeting (Participants' classifications)

Role	Behaviour	Details
Group blocking roles (Disruptive)	The aggressor	Deflates the status of others, disagrees and criticizes.
	The blocker or The arguer	Stubbornly disagrees, cites unrelated material or incorrect material, returns to the previous topics.
	The dominator	Tries to take over, asserts authority, manipulates the group.
	The person in rush	Paces the meeting faster by jumping through agenda; always in a hurry to finish; ignores the process compliance.
	The criticiser	Discourages or shows disregards for proceedings.
	The interrupter	Breaks the discussion to agree or disagree or make another point.
	The destroyer	Crushes any and every idea, can always find something wrong.
	The trapper	Waits for opportune moment to show error has been made—likes to raise questions to trap the Chairperson and participants
	The devil's advocate	More devil than advocate

Table 3.3: Disruptive behaviour in a meeting (Participants' classifications)

Role	Behaviour	Details
Casual Role	The playboy/girl	Shows off, tells funny stories, is nonchalant and cynical
	The chatterbox	Talks continually, rarely on the relevant topic, has a little to contribute

Table 3.4: Casual behaviour in a meeting (Participants' classifications)

Role	Behaviour	Details
Passive role	The withdrawer	Will not participate, engages in private conversations, takes copious personal notes.
	The special pleader	Draws attention to own concerns.
	The self-confessor	Talks irrelevantly of own feelings and insights.
	The sleeper	Uninterested in the proceedings; (some can sleep with eyes open!)

Table 3.5: Submissive behaviour in a meeting (Participants' classifications)

NLP has different view on behaviour. Let us look at NLP presuppositions.

People are not their behaviours—NLP suggests accepting a person, and a change in the person's behaviour can be possible (through coaching/counselling). Some people are not participating in a meeting because their confidence to speak is low. This may be due to their limiting belief. NLP has a belief that every participant has the capability to contribute. Positive change always comes from adding resources. In the example, the resource is confidence.

The meaning of all behaviour is dependent on the context—The meaning of the behaviour is clear when the context is understood. If someone sleeps in a meeting, then there can be another side. Speakers deliver an uninteresting and unexciting verbose in a usual boring staff meeting. The other reason could be that the meeting is at the end of a tiring day. We can understand the behaviour when the context is checked. Some people in a meeting disagree and block the discussion. Disagreement could be due to the concerns about the flaws or risks involved. This can be useful if discussion in a meeting was using a black hat (refer Appendix D). Thus, same behaviour can be useful when context is changed to 'black hat' thinking. The concerns could be addressed during 'green hat' thinking.

All behaviours have positive intention—The highest intention of behaviour will be to show gains. If a child breaks an electronic toy, the intention is his or her curiosity and learning. The behaviour observed is destructive; however, intention is positive. Some people in a meeting plead for a concern; we can ask why there is a concern. He or she is worried about the impact of a decision on the people, specially his or her group. We can ask why he or she worries. He or she wants the successful implementation of the decision. Though there are concerns and worries, the highest intention is positive, that is, successful implementation of the decision.

3.3   Motivation—Power, Affiliation, and Achievement

Meetings will be successful when the participants are motivated to give their opinion, make decisions, and take actions on decisions. David McClelland, a Harvard psychologist and an expert on motivation, stated that people are motivated by one of the following three things:

- Power and control
- Affiliation and popularity
- Achievement and success

We also know, in NLP, people are motivated either towards achievement or away from failures. This gives six categories for the meeting participants. We can use the same terms as per the participants' classification in Tables 3.1 to 3.5.

Power and control—Away

There are participants who do not have power to participate. The withdrawer takes plentiful personal notes and seldom talks. The sleeper is uninterested in the proceedings; some can sleep with eyes open! Wouldn't it be good to participate than to remain powerless?

Power and control—Towards

There are participants who have ability to control or set a direction. The elaborator builds on suggestions made by others. Tester raises questions to test if the group is ready to come to a decision or questions to raise important point that must be discussed.

Affiliation and popularity—Away

There are participants who wish to influence the meeting in a wrong way. The chatterbox talks continually but rarely talks on the topic. The playboy/girl shows off and is casual on discussion. Wouldn't it be good to focus on the purpose of the meeting than any diversion?

Affiliation and popularity—Towards

There are participants who are very helpful. The summariser pulls discussion together and reviews the progress so far. The harmoniser mediates the differences of opinion and reconciles the points of view. The encourager praises and supports others in their contributions.

Achievement and success—Away

There are participants who wish to get attention towards themselves. The recognition seeker boasts and talks excessively. The topic jumper continually changes the subject. Wouldn't it be good to have thoughtful contribution than wandering thoughts?

Achievement and success—Towards

There are participants who get attention because of their thoughtful contribution. The initiator suggests new/different ideas/approaches. The rationalist thinker makes worthwhile contributions through thought-out ideas.

A leader can motivate the participants with right motivation tactics.

3.4 Myers Briggs Type Indicator

A lot of literature is available on Myers Briggs Type Indicator (MBTI). It provides sixteen different personality types based on four parameters (as shown in Figure 3.1). Each parameter has two options. MBTI is one of the ways to look at different people, their working style, and their strengths. Each option has advantages in thinking, discussion, and decision-making. Some organisations use MBTI during recruitment, for example, ISTJ persons (introvert, sensing, thinking, judging) can be a good accountant. Marketing and sales job can be more suitable for ESTP persons (extrovert, sensing, thinking, perceiving). MBTI shows diversity among executives. The diversity in the meeting brings differing opinions and ideas that lead to more lively and interesting discussion, and, finally, the meetings can provide a creative solution and decision. The MBTI parameters and their types are as follows:

– Favourite world or energy source

- Introverted (I)—draws energy from inner world—information, thought, ideas, and other reflection—and requires 'private time' to recharge.
- Extraverted (E)—draws energy from outer world—people, places, and activities—and feels deprived if cut off from interaction with outside world.

– Information

- Sensing (S)—prefers clear and concrete data, information, facts, and figures and is comfortable with logic. However, dislikes fuzzy or ambiguous situations.
- Intuitive (N)—prefers imagination, patterns, and big picture and is comfortable with ambiguity.

– Decision-making

- Thinking (T)—looks at the logic in decision and required tasks and accepts conflicts as natural.
- Feeling (F)—considers feelings and impact on people and seeks consensus and popular opinion.

– Structure or day-to-day lifestyle

- Judging (J)—Plans and focuses on tasks and avoids stress due to deadlines.
- Perceiving (P)—acts without plan, does multitasking, and works best when close to deadline.

	Sensing (S)		Intuitive (N)		
Introverted	ISTJ	ISFJ	INFJ	INTJ	Judging (J)
(I)	ISTP	ISFP	INFP	INTP	Perceiving
Extroverted	ESTP	ESFP	ENFP	ENTP	(P)
(E)	ESTJ	ESFJ	ENFJ	ENTJ	Judging (J)
	Thinking (T)	Feeling (F)		Thinking (T)	

Figure 3.1: MBTI—Sixteen combinations.

MBTI is only a guideline on preferences and is not a rule. We should not conclude that an introvert person does not like a meeting or will not participate in a meeting. Thinking person will have an understanding of people side also. Every participant has an ability to participate. If we look at six thinking hats' methodology (refer Appendix D), some participants may enjoy specific hats. From MBTI perspective, ISTJ with a talent for facts and figures may contribute well in white hat thinking. Optimistic ESFP should give the required optimism for yellow hat thinking. ENFJ/INFJ will have a say on people's emotional reaction (red hat thinking). INFP/ENFP can bring creativity in green hat thinking. ESTJ/ENTJ can enforce process control required for blue hat thinking. To conclude, a leader should look for diversity and bring them together for the common purpose of the meeting.

3.5   Communication Style and Thinking Style

Every person has a lead representational system and a primary or preferred representational system. People use the primary representational system to store the information in their brain and use the lead representational to access the information from their brain. The general three representational systems are visual, auditory, and kinaesthetic. One or two representational systems can be dominant.

Visual—Visual people would like to see the things. Examples of language (linguistic predicates) used by a visual person to express an opinion are the following:

- 'I wish to get a big *picture* about . . .'
- 'Let us *look* at the figures.'

- 'I appreciate your *views* about . . .'

A visual person will be comfortable if we use graphs, charts, or illustrations in the meeting.

Auditory—Auditory people would like to hear the things. Examples of language (linguistic predicates) used by auditory person to express an opinion are the following:

- 'I wish to *hear* at higher scale . . .'
- '*Listen*, the figures are . . .'
- 'I understand what you want to *say*.'

Auditory person will like a brief explanation in the beginning, summary of the points, and summary of the conclusion.

Kinaesthetic—Kinaesthetic people would like to feel. Examples of language (linguistic predicates) used by kinaesthetic person to express an opinion are the following:

- 'I wish to get a *feel* of larger size . . .'
- 'Let us *read* the figures.'
- 'I can *sense* your point.'

Kinaesthetic person will like activities in a meeting, for example, writing points on flip charts or demonstration.

In case of one-to-one meetings, a person can match the representational system of other person, create rapport, and then lead to the required results.

In case of group meeting, it is good to follow K-A-V pattern (kinaesthetic, auditory, and visual). Kinaesthetic persons get attention with activity. Auditory persons get attention through introduction in the opening. Visual persons get attention through their presence of participants.

When people think, two things can happen—people remember from a past experience or construct a new thing in mind. This will also be done as per visual-auditory-kinaesthetic pattern. For example, a team is planning an offsite meeting. Different team member will have different thoughts. A team member will remember an image of the venue of the last meeting (visual remembered); another team member will construct an image of the venue of the upcoming meeting (visual constructed). A team member will remember the manager's speech/voice (auditory remembered); another team member will construct the discussion (audio) expected in the forthcoming meeting (auditory constructed). Some team member may remember the pat and congratulatory handshakes for his presentation (kinaesthetic). Thus, every participant of the meeting can have different thinking style.

In-depth learning of representation systems is covered in NLP practitioner course.

3.6   Information Processing Perspective

In a meeting, participants process the information. There are different ways people understand the information, and then they process the information.

In case of information, some people prefer to have big picture or summary, whereas some people prefer to have details.

'Big picture' people have comfort with abstract things, general picture, global view, or high-level purpose. Senior management people tend to fall under this category. Their participation in the meeting should be taken care with high-level presentation.

'Details' people will have questions as they will look for specifics. Meetings with these people should address finer points and bring clarity.

In case of understanding, some people will look for sameness, whereas some people will look for differences.

In a meeting, if we have the 'sameness' participants, then they will be comfortable with focus on commonality and will focus less on changes. This approach will help to manage the resistance for change.

In a meeting, if we have 'difference' participants, then they will be excited for the changes. They will be eager to look at the differences or mismatch and focus less on matching or commonality. We can plan the meeting and provide the information in such a way that their motivation remains high.

3.7   Team Perspective

We work in a team. The team could be a functional team, cross-functional team, or virtual team. Team players are the key to a successful team and successful organisation. Team meetings are a communication medium, and the style of the team player will have impact on meetings.

Glenn M. Parker classified team players into the following four categories:

- Contributors are task-oriented team members. Their strengths are high performance standard, well organised, and responsible. In a meeting, they can contribute information and data (white hat thinking).
- Collaborators are goal-directed team members. Their strength is their ability to see big picture and their good understanding of vision and mission. In a meeting, they provide forward-looking insight and imagination.
- Communicators are process-oriented team members. Their strength is they are active listeners and good facilitators and are able to build consensus and resolve conflicts. In a meeting, they can be a facilitator.
- Challengers are members who question. Their strength is being outspoken and thorough on subject. In a meeting, they can bring challenges.

3.8   Group Perspective

MBTI classification and representation systems are for individuals. It is also good to know group behaviour. In case of a project, a group is formed and is adjourned at the end of the project. The group moves through forming, storming, and norming stages before it reaches a performing stage. Table 3.6 shows the characteristics of each group stage and its relevance to the meeting. Generally, a group cannot escape any stage to reach the performing stage. A leader should aim to lead the group to the performing stage.

Stage	Characteristics	Meeting aspects
Forming	Testing behaviour of individuals, interrelationship, and interdependence.	Very positive at the initial meetings Focused on task orientation and ground rules
Storming	Subgroups formation, Arguments and disagreements, and Lack of unity	Handling the conflicts Challenges for productivity and quality improvement
Norming	Resistance overcome and Cohesive group	Open communication. Constructive criticism. Very positive outcome
Performing	Flexibility, Group synergy, and SMART Goals	Participative leadership Self-managed team

Table 3.6: Group stages

Many groups may not reach the performing stage. It is possible that the group may fall back to lower stages (forming or storming) due to changes in the team members or changes in the processes.

Leaders will have challenges in conducting a meeting at forming and storming stages. The leader and the participants should consider the following NLP presuppositions:

Everyone has a unique model of the world—Everyone is unique because of the experiences and knowledge gathered over the years and talent developed over the years. Every participant in the meeting is unique.

Respect the model of the world of other people—This means respect others or appreciate others. However, it does not mean you need to agree for everything in the meeting.

People with more flexibility in their behaviours will have greater influence over others—Flexibility gives connectivity with different people. A person with flexibility presents his or her points in non-dogmatic way.

Resistance in a person/group is due to lack of rapport—Rapport builds trust. Lack of rapport means lack of trust. Lack of trust is seen in the form of resistance.

Positive worth of an individual is held constant, while the value and appropriateness of internal and/or external behaviour is questioned—Positivity about self-worth and positivity in others will help to appreciate the talent in everyone.

3.9   Globalisation Perspective

Globalisation has brought people together from different parts of the world with different cultures. Culture influences the working style, interaction between leaders and subordinates, communication, and meeting style. Every country has its own culture, and subcontinent-size countries like China, India, and USA, and so on have different cultures within the country. However, when we think globally, we often divide culture into two—eastern culture and western culture.

There are generalised differences between eastern and western cultures. Westerners are more focused on tasks, whereas easterners will look for relationship building. Westerners will prefer direct talk and explicit message. Easterners will use indirect language and implicit message. Easterners are more status conscious. For example, let a senior person start the meeting or let the leader introduce the participants of the meeting. Westerners show egalitarianism by presenting his or her self. They look for individual achievement and have independent working style. Easterners look for group's achievement and show interdependence.

Most of the people would like to be appreciated for their culture. This will show your interest in them. It will be good to learn things in their language, for example, greetings and phrases for courtesy like 'thank you'. It may be audio conference or videoconference or meetings during foreign visit. You can have knowledge of their culture to make a meeting effective. (Aperian Global, www.aperianglobal.com, provides training program on global leadership with detailed information on country specific culture)

3.10 Continuum Perspective

The behaviour, working style, and preferences can be seen on a continuum. These aspects have been discussed in the previous sections. Figure 3.2 shows the different continuums. Each continuum shows two polarities, and people may fall anywhere on the continuum. Various aspects are useful to understand yourself as well as others. This is very useful in communication and building rapport and relationship. These aspects may change from situation to situation and from time to time.

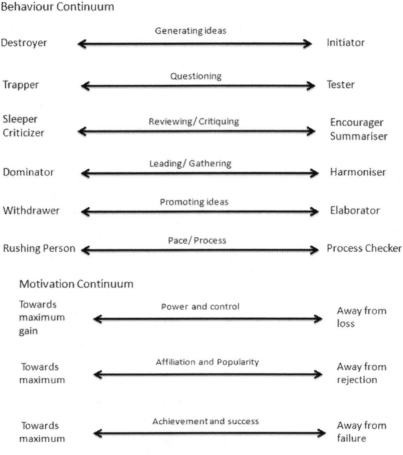

Figure 3.2: Continuum showing polarities.

Figure 3.2: Continuum showing polarities (continued).

3.11 Challenges

Most of the books on meetings consider handling of disruptive behaviours as challenges. The solutions for these behaviours are shown in Table 3.7. These may work temporarily as the participant may continue with the same undesirable behaviour.

Behaviour(s)	Handling the situation
Aggressor Dominator	• Set the ground rules for the meeting so that participation from everyone is ensured. • Process compliance (For example, in case six thinking hats methodology, point raised must be relevant to a specific hat) • Redirect discussion to other participants "We all recognise your expertise, let us hear from other participants"
Blocker Destroyer	• Process compliance (For example, In case of six thinking hats methodology, negative points will be discussed under black hat, park your point for a while, raise it during discussion on black hat thinking) • Acknowledge the main point; thank for raising the point; invite comments from other participants; find the merit; express agreement and move on
Withdrawer Sleeper (silent type)	• Ask a question you are confident that the participant can easily answer • Engage them by calling their name and asking their opinion • Say words of encouragement for the participation
Chatterbox Know All	• When these type of participants take a pause, immediately say, "Thank for your comments. Let us hear from others" • When these types of participants keep repeating the same thing in different way, interrupt and say, "Excuse me. I need to interrupt you. Everyone understood your point. Let us hear the comments from others."
Playboy/ girl	• Set the ground rules for the meeting e.g. dress code • Guide them and develop them as the tension reliever

Table 3.7: Handling disruptive behaviours.

However, NLP emphasises on effective communication and rapport building. NLP suggests leading the participants to ideal behaviour. The NLP presuppositions discussed in the previous sections are useful. A list of all NLP presuppositions are given in Appendix B.

A challenge is to align individuals for common purpose of meetings with synergy.

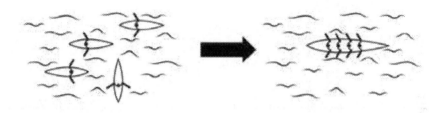

3.12 Synergy

Stephen Covey's sixth habit is synergy. It is the culmination of all other habits, especially habit 4, 'think win/win', and habit 5, 'seek first to understand, then to be understood'.

Synergy will be experienced when a group reaches the stage of performing. Communication is open, transparent (no hidden motives), and absolutely with trust. The team respects individual team members (respect other person's model of the world) and value the diversity among the team members (e.g. MBTI, cultural diversity, and representational system). The team shares the same values, and there is positivity in goals, mission, and vision (neurological levels). These motivate the team. Motivated team displays and exercises the required coordination. Peak performance shows efficiency, effectiveness, and energy; it is achieved through systems, strategies, and synergy.

3.13 More from NLP

NLP master practitioner includes more topics on people working style. More than 50 meta programmes have been identified. We looked at a couple of them (information receiving and processing). The meta programmes explain why two persons under same MBTI classification are different.

Prof. Clare W. Graves (professor in psychology) developed the spiral dynamics theory to provide an idea on how the values and ethics have been evolved in the society.

These are useful to enhance the understanding of people and utilise them in meetings.

3.14 In summary

Having essential participants and their contributions makes the meetings effective, efficient, and energetic. Business processes can help to determine the required participants. Neurological level also provides the required level of discussion and corresponding level of participants. Another important aspect is to understand the participants, their working style, their motivation, their communication style, their culture, and so on. As per NLP presuppositions, people are not their behaviours; there is positive worth in them. Meetings can bring their peak performance through effective communication and good understanding of their working style.

As a part of a system, we looked at the psychometric parameters to know the participants well.

Our strategy is to tackle undesirable behaviour through tactful language. This is short-term measure. For long-term, our strategy is to see changes in behaviour.

Better understanding of each other and understanding among all help to build synergy.

3.15 Afterthought

After going through this chapter, you will have thoughts about the discussion in this chapter. Our theme is to build the systems, strategies and synergies for the meetings. With due respect to your model of the world, please jot down your thoughts on systems, strategies and synergies.

- What are the systems needed for a meeting?

_____

_____

_____

- What are the strategies required for a meeting?

_____

_____

_____

- How are the synergies built for a meeting?

_____

_____

_____

MEETING GAME PREPARATION

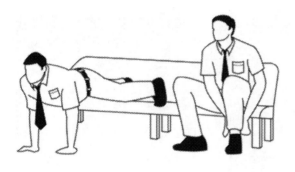

4. How Do I Plan and Prepare for the Meeting?

Benjamin Franklin said, 'By failing to prepare, you are preparing to fail.' This is true for meetings. Meeting preparation is the foundation for the successful meeting. Organisations should have more planned meetings and very few emergency meetings.

Athletes prepare physically and mentally for sports event. In case of cricket, players will do net practice and look after physical fitness and diet. In case of soccer, players will practise passing and shooting and warm-up for the match. Sports team will also work out the strategies. Similarly, meetings need mental (strategies, presentations, and so on) and physical preparation (facilities).

Meeting planning covers the administrative part, the facility, and an agenda of the meeting. Based on the agenda, the leader, the facilitator, and the participants will prepare for the meeting. This should answer the questions: where the meeting will take place, at what time, and what are the points for the discussion.

4.1   Participants' Availability (2/3 Rule)

This is the first check. When the participants to be invited are confirmed and the time required for a meeting is estimated, the availability of all participants is checked. Meeting schedule will confirm the following:

- 2/3 agenda items are applicable to all participants.
- 2/3 participants must have confirmed their attendance.

If this is not satisfied, then revise the agenda and/or reschedule the meeting. It is good to maximise the attendance and participation.

4.2   Facility Planning

Admin officer should select convenient venue based on the number of participants. One-to-one meetings can happen in a cabin, whereas conference of hundred sales representatives will need careful selection of larger venue. If the people are travelling from distance, then the venue should be well connected to reach. If the meeting is planned as an off-site event, then transport arrangements will be required. Admin officer should ensure the meeting place where only business will take place. For example, staff meeting in a canteen will not be appropriate.

It is also necessary to look at arrangements in the meeting room. These arrangements will have impact on interaction or participation. From NLP angle, it is preferred that all participants see each other so that non-verbal communication (body language) can be observed. Figure 4.1 shows the typical seating arrangements for the meeting.

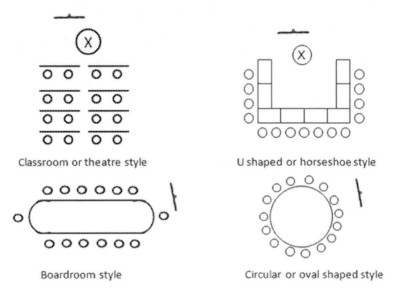

Figure 4.1: Different seating arrangements for a meeting

Classroom style or theatre style: A leader will have great power by taking position. All can see the presentation screen easily and clearly. There can be a minimal interruption for the leader. Talking among the participants will be minimal. This type of meeting arrangement may be good for addressing large group. The major disadvantage is that it is not conducive for participation.

U-shaped style or horseshoe style: This offers equality among the participants. The leader is in centre with full control and eye contact with all the participants. Visual aids have clear visibility. When participants interact with other participants, it can be distracting. It has minimal space utilisation. A weak leader or a spineless boss may feel pressure at the centre.

Circular or oval shaped style: Equality is stressed. The leader and the participants are together with great visibility of other participants. The non-verbal communication is feasible. This type of room arrangement is excellent for participation. However, visual aid may not have a good location as some participants can have discomfort.

Boardroom style: This is used by senior management. Table is square or oval shape, suitable for 10-12 people.

Other facilities will include as per the following requirements:

- Flipchart or whiteboard to write or display ideas
- Marking pens for flipchart/whiteboard
- Laptop or desktop for use of PowerPoint slides or use of intranet and internet or use of web conferencing
- Projector and presentation screen or display unit
- Telephone for teleconference
- Videoconference equipment for videoconference

Office chairs are ergonomically designed for comfort of the participants. The room should have proper lighting and air conditioning or heating. However, it is good to have sunlight and fresh air. It saves energy bills as well as it provides natural energy to the meeting participants.

Day-long meetings will need arrangement for food and refreshment. Meeting rooms should have access to pantry for refreshment, or keeping chocolates or candies in the meeting room can be a good idea. This is good for kinaesthetic persons as there is gustatory (taste) and olfactory (smell) experience.

The software like Microsoft Outlook allows the administrator to book facilities within the organisation and the participants' calendar.

4.3 Meeting Roles

Meeting roles have been discussed in a process definition in Chapter 1. Depending on the number of participants, roles can be assigned. A leader will initiate the meeting. Facilitator and secretary (recorder) are the key roles. If it is feasible, someone can attend the meeting in the capacity of these roles. Sometimes, a leader may have reservation to delegate these roles due to confidentiality reason. The role of a facilitator is discussed in Chapter 8.

Some organisations assign the roles on rotation so that everyone gets equal opportunity. It is good to assign the roles in advance to avoid any confusion. Typical roles and responsibilities are given in Table 4.1. From the perspective of meeting preparation, the leader, facilitator and participants must do the required preparation.

In case of global meetings, all participants may not be English speaking; there can be a role of an interpreter, who knows both languages and can explain the on-going discussion.

Role	Responsibilities
Leader	• Define the purpose, set objective, give direction
Facilitator	• Plan and coordinate meeting • Prepare for the meeting • Facilitate the discussion • Manage the meeting process
Participants	• Prepare for the meeting • Contribute to meeting discussion • Take up the task decided • Complete tasks
Note-taker/Secretary	• Write up agenda and distribute prior to the meeting • Take notes with key points during the meeting • Write up minutes of meeting and distribute
Time keeper	• Monitor the time for agenda items • Indicate the warning signals, if required

Table 4.1: Roles and responsibilities.

From discussion perspective, the participants need to take different roles.

Robert Dilts, who has contributed a lot to NLP, suggested the following three roles based on research on successful entrepreneurs:

- Dreamer—a leader with vision (green hat is useful)
- Realist—acts on the ideas or implementer and will have positive perception (yellow hat is useful)
- Critics—identifies problems and risks (black hat is useful)

Meetings progress from planning to conducting and finally implementing actions. Hence, it is team work, and team role can be useful for understanding the roles in the whole process. Dr Meridith Belbin suggested very comprehensive model for team roles (more information is on http://www.belbin.com).

The social aspects are covered by the following people:

- Coordinator—facilitates and brings balance
- Resources investigator—finds opportunities and information and develops network
- Team worker—supports

The thinking aspects are covered by the following people:

- Plant—generates ideas and solves problem
- Specialist—provides expert advice
- Monitor evaluator—evaluates and judges

The action aspects are covered by the following people:

- Shaper—leads and helps in overcoming obstacles
- Implementer—organises and gets it done
- Completer/Finisher—thinks in details and finishes with perfection

These roles are preferences of team members. As mentioned in Chapter 3, we should not label any person. All are capable of playing different roles.

4.4   Preparation with Six Thinking Hats

When an organisation is using 'Six thinking hats' methodology, two hats are in action to plan and prepare for the meeting. Blue hat thinking is used in planning, and white hat thinking is used for providing information.

Blue hat thinking: This is a control hat. The control starts with a plan for a meeting. This will determine how different hats will be used or their sequence. Minor variation is permitted based on the outcome.

White hat thinking: This is a hat for information. All the available information—facts and figure—are given to the participants so that they can prepare for the meeting. This also means that the participants need to collect necessary information for the white hat session during the meeting. White hat thinking also identifies missing data or information. This prepares participant for what to ask.

4.5   Strategy: NLP Concept

A strategy (in NLP) is a sequence of thought and behaviour based on a set of belief and sense of self to accomplish a specific outcome. It is what we do in our mind that lets us do things in our reality. In NLP terms, strategy is the order and sequence of internal and external representation (refer Appendix A) that leads to a specific outcome. We have already introduced representation in Chapter 3 (Section 3.5).

A leader/facilitator should work on strategies for the meeting. Having no strategy is a bad strategy. This means that strategy of unconscious mind (and his/her preferred representation system) is not known to the person. Hence, he may not be able to participate constructively in the meeting. Having negative strategy is a worst strategy for the success of the meeting.

Let us look at negative strategy.

- There will be boring presentation(s). The boss will give routine advices.
- I will carry my laptop and will check emails.
- If I miss something in the meeting, I will read the minutes of the meeting.

This type of negative strategy will lead to a poor participation, and success of the meeting is ruined.

The purpose indicates the desired outcome of the meeting. Strategy needs to be planned for the desired outcome. If the meeting is with a customer, then sales team can work on sales strategy. If there will be negotiations, then the team will work on negotiation strategy. If a leader wishes to motivate the team, he or she should work on motivation strategy. In reality, the leader must have motivational strategy for every meeting so that the participants will be energised in the meeting to take actions.

For example, an IT manager had a strategy for problem solution meeting.

- I would like to hear the problem statement (audio).
- I would like to see system components and interconnections (visual).
- I would like to listen to the team's solution option (audio). I would like to talk to myself and visualise (audio and visual).
- I would like to write clear steps for the actions to solve the problem (kinaesthetic).

Trigger for above strategy is a problem raised to the IT manager. The IT manager operates based on his strategy, and problem solution is tested. If the IT manager is not satisfied, new solution is sought. If the IT manager is satisfied, there is exit from the strategy to take actions in reality.

Important presupposition is 'if what you are doing (your strategy) is not working, do something else (develop new strategy)'.

As a part of meeting preparation, the leader and the participants should have a strategy in terms of what they would like to hear, see, and feel.

Stephen Covey's second habit is 'begin with the end in mind'. Everything is created in the mind first, and then it actually happens. By having a strategy with reference to your preferred representational system, the leader can have a meeting in the mind first and have successful meeting with the habit of 'begin with the end in mind'.

4.6　Agenda Preparation

An agenda is prepared by extending the purpose in terms of items and sequencing them with time allocation. This will provide input to the participants to prepare for the meeting. The agenda is also considered as a control tool to prevent any diversion during the meeting and bring back to focus on the purpose of the meeting.

Some organisations have regular meetings, and agenda items are invited. This may result in heterogeneous items with no common specific purpose. Hence, it is good to have a clear purpose for the meeting as discussed in Chapter 2, and agenda items should be related to the purpose.

Time is allocated for each item on an agenda. Time allocation should consider time for presentation, time for discussion, time for voting, and time needed for agreement. It is good to have some flexibility in time allocation. However, the start time and end time are clearly defined. Schedule time (start and end) should indicate correct time zone whether it is Indian Standard Time or GMT or specific US time zone. Any miscommunication will have an impact on the participation. Long meetings (three hours or more) should include appropriate number of breaks.

Some organisations follow bell-shaped agenda (normal curve). This agenda will have simple items in the beginning, followed by tough or hard items, and ends with simple item.

The draft agenda with purpose statement can be circulated to the key participants. The agenda can be revised based on the feedback.

4.7　Agenda Items

Agenda items are the outcomes desired to achieve the purpose. The outcomes or goals are suggested to be SMART (specific, measurable, attainable, realistic, and timely). SMART parameters can be clearly decided during the meeting. However, agenda item should be expressed as actionable item and specific. Action verb with specificity makes agenda actionable. For example, agenda item 'discussion on design' will be ambiguous. Agenda item 'review of AAA design version 1.1 for technical feasibility' will provide clarity and the participants will have minimal assumptions. Participants can also refer to specific document and prepare well for the meeting.

4.8   Meeting Agenda Communication

The leader/facilitator should ensure the distribution of the agenda well in advance before the meeting. This will help them to have sufficient time to prepare for the meeting. If an organisation has a standard format/form for agenda, follow that format so that all required content will be included in the meeting agenda.

During the meeting, emphasis should be placed more on information processing than providing information. Hence, providing information should take place before the meeting as much as possible.

Agenda communication is an opportunity to establish a rapport with the participants. The meeting invitation email can use a language based on the preferred representation system—visual, auditory, or kinaesthetic (refer Section 3.5) of the participants. Meetings invite should avoid jargons and should consider model of the world of participants so that communication is clear. This makes sure that the purpose of the meeting is understood by all participants.

4.9   Presentation Preparation

The leader/participant may need to prepare presentations for the meeting. The facilitator should inform the time allocated for the presentation (agenda item), or sometimes the limit on the number of slides is mentioned. As many executives have a lot of information to share, presentation exceeds the slide limit or too much of text (information) is crammed in the slides. This will lead to unsuccessful meetings.

Good practice on slide preparation is having maximum six rows with six words in each line. This will give optimum chunk size to grasp.

Guidelines for presentation format (by Bernice McCarthy) is as follows:

- Why—explain need and relevance
- What—explain concept
- How—explain practical aspect
- What if—discuss different scenario

4.10 In Summary

Meeting preparations lays the foundation for successful meetings. Lack of preparation will result in lack of effectiveness, efficiency, and energy.

On administration front, it is booking the facilities and others things like travel and food.

Meeting role takers need to prepare for the meeting. They should have strategy. Overall meeting preparation is shown in Figure 4.2.

In case of a system, we looked at the tools like booking of required facility, strategy, and presentation in meeting preparation.

In case of strategies, we adopted 2/3 rule for availability and participation. For meeting preparation, strategy is to begin with the end in mind.

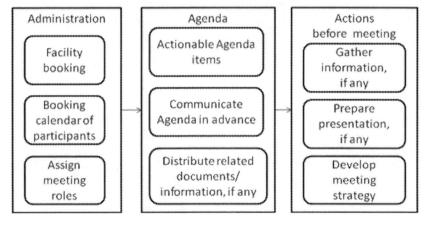

Figure 4.2: Meeting preparation.

In case of synergy, the agenda communication is an opportunity to set rapport and motivate towards the purpose of the meeting.

4.11 Afterthought

After going through this chapter, you will have thoughts about the discussion in this chapter. Our theme is to build the systems, strategies and synergies for the meetings. With due respect to your model of the world, please jot down your thoughts on systems, strategies and synergies.

- What are the systems needed for a meeting?

_____

_____

_____

- What are the strategies required for a meeting?

_____

_____

_____

How are the synergies built for a meeting?

_____

_____

_____

MEETING GAME IN PROGRESS

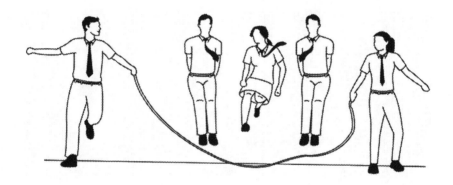

5. How Do I Conduct a Meeting?

John Christian Bovee said, 'The method of the enterprising is to plan with audacity and execute with vigour.' This is applicable to meetings. The planning and preparation was discussed in Chapter 4. This chapter is about the execution of a meeting plan.

A meeting is like a sport event. Sports persons will execute their plan during the event; however, they are alert or observant on how the event unfolds. They take decision based on current situations. They will choose to attack or defend without forgetting the purpose.

As the meeting unfolds, discussion will take place; new ideas and new situations will be explored without moving away from the purpose of the meeting.

This chapter is more from a leader or a facilitator's perspective. However, these points are useful for all the participants of the meeting. First part of this chapter addresses how to be attentive and establish rapport and then discusses the opening of the meeting and discussion. Discussions should lead to decisions and action items.

5.1 Be Observant

A leader and a participant must be attentive, and this is applicable to verbal as well as non-verbal communication. In NLP, it is called sensory acuity. Different cues are just indicators and are not rigid rules.

Linguistic predicates

We have seen preferred representation system in Chapter 3 (Section 3.5). We need to develop observation skills to make out their preferred representation system (auditory, visual, or kinaesthetic), and then we can also make out their strategy. We need to notice their language or the linguistic predicates used to understand the preferred representation system.

Eye Accessing Cues

Another cue is eye accessing pattern. The eyes (pupil of the eye) will move in a certain direction. This will indicate whether a person is constructing or remembering. Table 5.1, 5.2 and 5.3 show the moment of eye with reference to a person's thinking. This is for normally organised person (majority of people). There are some reversed organised persons also.

Eye movement	Question and representation
	Eyes will move to side left when we remember a sound or hear word(s). If we ask, 'Who has the softest voice in our team?', the team member will recall or remember the voice and then answer. (Auditory recall).
	Eyes will move to side right when we construct a sound. If we ask, 'How would you sound giving presentation in the next sales conference?', the person will construct the voice to listen. (Auditory constructed).

Table 5.1: Auditory eye accessing cues

Eye movement	Question and representation
	Eyes will move to downright when we are accessing touch, taste, smell, and feelings. If we ask, 'What was the feeling when the audience applauded for you?', the person will access the feelings. (Kinaesthetic).
	Eyes will move to down left when we talk to ourselves, that is, internal dialogue. If we ask, 'What would you say if you win this contest?', the person will have an internal dialogue. (Auditory digital—self talk).

Table 5.2: Eye accessing cues (Kinaesthetic and self-talk)

Eye movement	Question and representation
	Eyes will move to up right when we construct a picture or imagine a picture. If we say, 'Propose better seating arrangement in the office space to accommodate new staff', the person will construct a picture of the office space. (Visual construction).
	Eyes will move to up left when we remember a picture. If we ask, 'Which is the biggest meeting room to accommodate our team?', the team member will remember the rooms and then answers. (Visual remembered).
	Sometimes some people look straight ahead in defocused way. This is also visualising. It may appear as a glazed look.

Table 5.3: Visual eye accessing cues

Physiological cues

We may be able to recognise the representational system by observing physiology.

Let us look at the postures and body types of different persons.

Visual persons may have straight back, head looking up, hunched shoulders, and gestures high up. They may have fingers and arms extended. Their body type may be thin with tensed body, and the skin colour may be pale.

Kinaesthetic persons may slouch or bend over. Shoulders may tend to droop. Head sits solidly on the shoulders, and palms may be upturned. Kinaesthetic internal type person (internal means mental feeling) will have a soft body. Kinaesthetic external type person (external means feeling action or physical senses) will have muscular body and will have athletic posture. Skin colour may be more colourful and redder or shiny.

Auditory person will have head on one side and may point to ears. An auditory external will lean forward, whereas an auditory internal will lean back. Arms may be folded. Auditory persons will tend to have body between kinaesthetic persons (soft) and visual persons (tense). The auditory external tends to soften, whereas the auditory internal tends to tighten. Skin colour of the auditory person can be normal or pale.

Voice cues

Voice cues are about tonality, tempo, and timbre. Visual persons may have fast tempo, high pitch, and nasal tonality. Kinaesthetic persons may have slow tempo with long pauses and have low and deep tonality. An auditory person's voice may be melodic and rhythmic with clear diction. An auditory internal will have monotone, same pitch, and robot-like tonality.

Breathing cue

Visual persons may have shallow breathing. Breathing is high in chest. Kinaesthetic persons may have deep breathing. It is low in the stomach area. Auditory persons may have even breathing in the diaphragm or with the whole chest.

Observation in a meeting

As people enter in the meeting room, we should make a sensory check and understand their physiology. The leader/facilitator can check that the meeting has alert and responsive participants.

Important rule is, we should not label people or have prejudices. If someone is folding hands, we should not make judgement that the person as 'not an open' person. It may be possible that he or she is uncomfortable with the temperature (cold) of the room.

A person may breathe heavily for excitement, whereas other person may breathe heavily for anger. That means we need to be careful in observing the persons and sensing the feelings.

NLP suggests calibrating persons based on their physiology and state of mind. In a meeting, one person says yes with physiology indicating yes, whereas another person says yes with physiology indicating no. The leader/facilitator should not ignore the second person; effective communication happens when people fully agree verbally and non-verbally.

In case of face-to-face meeting, all the cues can be used. In case of audio conference, voice cues and linguistic cues can be used.

5.2 Opening the Meeting

Opening of the meeting will set the stage for the meeting. However, few things should be checked either by administrator or facilitator.

- Meeting room is clean and set up for the meeting. There are sufficient chairs arranged in required style.
- Other equipment—projector, laptop/desktop, board, flipchart, and coloured marker pen are available.
- In case of a teleconference, telephone equipment is checked, and the facilitator can dial-in early so that he or she can welcome the participants.
- In case of a videoconference, ensure the equipment is checked, and the facilitator can login early to welcome the participants.

Some of the good practices in opening the meeting are as follows:

- Welcoming the participants: The leader/facilitator will welcome the participants. If meeting participants are across the globe, we should take care of the timing (it is morning in US, afternoon in UK, and evening in India). If participants do not know each other (and are less than ten in number), there can be a quick introduction of the participants.
- Confirm the agenda and the purpose: The leader/facilitator will have an opening address, stating the purpose and agenda. If there is any change in the agenda, then mention the change. The purpose and outcomes are made clear to all so that there will be no hidden agenda. The leader should lead the team to resourceful states (motivated, humorous, at ease, committed, energised, and so on). Building rapport is discussed in the next session.
- Establish timeframe: The leader/facilitator will inform the timeframe for the meeting and the outcome, if necessary. The organisation and the leader should practise starting the meeting on time. Agreed timeframe will help to finish meetings in time.
- Confirm the roles: The leader/facilitator ensures that the role takers (timer or note taker) are in the meeting or mention the changes, if any.
- Establish ground rule: The organisation will have meeting norms, and some of them will be related to security/confidentiality,

for example, only one person talking at a time, confidential information 'staying in the room', cell-phone on silent mode, and so on. The facilitator can mention the ground rules at the beginning of the meeting.

5.3   Establishing Rapport

Meetings will be successful if there is a rapport among the participants. Good rapport will give enjoyable experience, whereas lack of rapport will lead to frustrating experience. Rapport was discussed briefly in Chapter 3 (Section 3.5). Key aspects are, we should maintain respect for each other (probably many organisations have this as a value), recognise the contribution the participants are going to make, and reassure (motivate) that the purpose of the meeting is achieved.

NLP's mantra for rapport is 'Really All People Prefer Others Resembling Themselves'. We look commonality with other person(s). The commonality could be verbal or non-verbal. As the communication happens 55 per cent through body language, 38 per cent through vocal qualities, and 7 per cent through words, rapport also has the same percentage.

As per NLP, mind and body are linked through language. Mind reflects on body (physiology) and vice versa. When we match our body language with body language of other person, our thinking also matches and rapport is built.

Physiology covers posture (sitting or standing) and gestures (facial expression, eye contact, breathing, and so on).

Voice quality covers tone (high pitch or low pitch), tempo (fast or slow), and volume (loud or soft).

Matching and mirroring

Matching means doing exactly the same thing. If first person touches his cheek with left hand and second person touches his cheek with left hand, then the second person is matching. If the first person touches his cheek with left hand and the second person touches his cheek with right hand (mirror image), then the second person is mirroring (Figure 5.1). Matching and mirroring are not mimicry. It is done in subtle way and in a discrete manner (with delay of few seconds) to express an empathy through body language.

Figure 5.1: Matching and mirroring.

Pacing and leading

Pacing a person means following a person using matching or mirroring. For example, person A (kinaesthetic) will match person B (auditory) through physiology and/or vocal quality and/or words with person B's representation system—auditory. This will establish rapport between A and B. This means both persons A and B are in sync at subconscious level.

Second part is leading. In this example, it is assumed that person A knows how persons A and B wish to achieve the outcome. Once the rapport is established, person A will start using his representation system (kinaesthetic) and person B will start following. In other words, person A is now leading. Thus, person A can convince person B, achieving the desired outcome.

In a meeting, the leader needs to pace the participants and then lead them to desired outcome.

5.4 Discussion

If meeting planning and preparation forms the backbone of a meeting, then heart of the meeting is the discussion to process information and to make a decision(s). Ideally, all information should be received prior to the meeting. However, there is a possibility that meetings may provide information and then process it. Meeting participants will gather information and present it in the meeting. The presentations can be on a problem or proposal for the discussion. The facilitator needs to control the information flow or discussion and arrive at a conclusion. Discussion is stimulated through questions—open-ended questions, redirected questions, paraphrased questions, and clarifying questions. We can explore NLP concepts related to discussion.

Hierarchy of ideas

Hierarchy of ideas indicates the level of discussion or direction. The term *chunk up* means moving to an abstract level. In case of a meeting, we have the purpose of the meeting (abstract level). In case of an organisation, the highest level to chunk up can be the vision of the organisation. The term *chunk down* means moving to the details. In case of a meeting, we go into specific details on the subject during the meeting. The term *chunk laterally* means the same level with another alternative or similar thing.

These concepts can be viewed for IT departments.

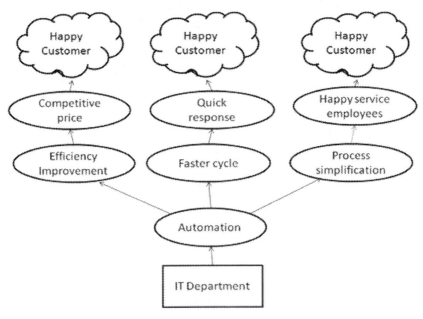

Figure 5.2: Chunk-up.

Figure 5.2 shows chunk-up for IT department. IT department aims for automation. The purpose of automation could be improving efficiencies, reducing cycle time, or simplifying processes. This will lead to competitive price, quick response, or better service. The highest purpose of this will be to achieve customer satisfaction or happy customer. The purpose of happy customer will lead to organisation's mission/vision, and this ultimately shows the existence of the organisation.

Figure 5.3 shows Chunk-down for IT department. This asks what exactly IT department works on. First level of answer could be IT works on software and hardware.

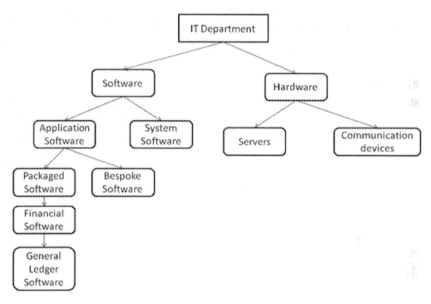

Figure 5.3: Chunk-down.

Further probing will give more details. Next level is application software and system software. Application software is further divided into packaged software and bespoke software. Specific packaged software can be financial software. More specific detail is general ledger module.

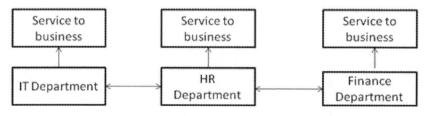

Figure 5.4: Chunk lateral to compare similar things.

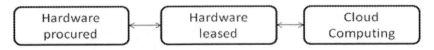

Figure 5.5: Chunk lateral to have alternatives.

Figures 5.4 and 5.5 show the chunk lateral. IT department, HR department, and finance department—all three departments provide services to business. There can be certain parameters which can be compared, for example, in-house cost versus out-sourcing cost.

Another example could be IT department exploring the cost of buying hardware, leasing hardware, or using cloud computing resources. This is chunking sideways to find alternatives.

In a meeting, if there is disagreement, facilitator can chunk up to higher level till disagreeing parties/participants understand the purpose or common goal and come to an agreement. When there is a need for clarity, the facilitator or participants can chunk down to obtain specific details.

Meta Model

Chunk-down gives the specificity through questions like who, what, where, which, how, how often, and so on. If we assess communication using NLP communication model (refer Appendix A), then we know people modify the message through deletion, distortion, and generalisation. Meta model has questioning techniques that bring up the missing element of the message. Some of the examples of statement (S) and related question (Q) are as follows:

– Deletion

- Simple deletion: S—'I am unhappy.' Q—'About what?'
- Simple deletion (unspecified relationship): S—'This problem is there for a long time and difficult to solve.' Q—'What is the relationship between time elapsed and difficulty in solution?'
- Comparative deletion: S—'If you make it more user friendly, then users will accept.' Q—'More than what?'/'Which specific areas?'
- Lack of referential index: S—'They do not entertain me.' Q—'Who specifically? When?'

- Unspecified verb: S—'He praised me.' Q—'How specifically praised?'
- Nominalisation: S—'There is no synergy.' Q—'Among whom? When? Where?'

– Distortion

- Mind reading: S—'You are wondering.' Q—'How do you know I am wondering?'
- Lost performance: S—'It is bad to be unrealistic.' Q—'Who says it is bad?'/'For whom it is bad?'/'How do you know that?'
- Complex equivalence: S—'Being late to the office means being irresponsible.' Q—'How does coming on time make someone responsible?'
- Cause and effect: S—'If you start early, you will finish first.' Q—'How does early start cause early finish?'
- Presupposition: S—'Boss is manipulative.' Q—'Are all bosses manipulative?'/'Are all the subordinates get manipulated?'/'How do you know that?'

– Generalisation

- Universal quantifier: S—'You always draw a wrong picture.' Q—'Always? Are all pictures wrong?'
- Modal operator (possibility): S—'He cannot work on this issue,' Q—'What prevents him?'
- Modal operator (necessary): S—'He must work late in the office.' Q—'What would happen if he did not?'

There is no 'why' question in meta model. 'Why' puts a person on defensive mode, and response could be excuses. Convergent questions—what, where, whom, who, and when bring the specifics. Kepner Treoge model for problem solving (refer Chapter 7) also avoids asking why.

Tony Robin, one of the top motivational speakers and authors, says that thinking is asking and answering the right question. In a meeting, participants ask and answer the question, and that takes them from confusion to clarity to achieve the outcome.

Outcome frame

Outcome frame focuses on the achievement of the meeting. In Chapter 2, we discussed the need for a meeting and converting the needs into purpose or outcome of the meeting. In Chapter 3, we looked at main resource of the meeting (that is, the participants) to achieve the outcome. In Chapter 4, we looked at expanding outcome frame in terms of agenda and also adding other resources like facilities.

During the meeting, the outcome frame is useful to check the relevance that is, how does the point or statement relate to the outcome of the meeting? This will be a check on diversion that can happen during the meeting.

Agreement frame

In a meeting, if participants agree on some point, conclude with decision (or action) and move on to the next point. The agreed points or levels form the agreement frame. This is very useful in negotiation and conflict resolution.

As discussed, when there is a disagreement, the facilitator can chunk up to agreement level so that the participants again will be in sync and ready to chunk down for details.

Rapport or pacing discussed in this chapter is the first step towards agreement (non-verbal agreement). Agreement will move forward when meeting participants use a positive and clean language. This means the participants will avoid using words *but* and *try*. If the participant says, 'I agree this point but . . .' this negates and shows disagreement. The participant can say, 'I agree and . . .' This is better option than using *but*. Similarly, if the participant says, 'I will try to complete . . .' this negates and shows disagreement on completion. The better option is 'I will complete on . . .' than using *try* and showing uncertainty about completion.

Useful ways of expressing points that support agreement frame are the following:

- 'I agree and . . .'
- 'I appreciate and . . .'
- 'I respect and . . .'

As-if frame

Meetings need divergent questions and divergent thinking. As-if frame helps to do that. The following are some of the examples:

— A meeting is for project planning. The facilitator will ask the team to imagine that *as if* project is completed successfully. Then

  • What are the steps needed to complete the project?
  • What are the learning points from this completed project?

  This imagination with 'as-if frame' makes the project planning more thoroughly.

— A meeting is for IT strategy. The facilitator will ask the participants to imagine that as if they are board members reviewing IT strategy. Then

  • What are the questions on IT strategy?
  • With imagination and putting yourself in other's shoe, participants can deliver acceptable strategy.

Ecology frame

This is an ecology check. Simple questions can be the following:

  • Are outcomes (of the meeting) safe to us?
  • Are outcomes (of the meeting) safe to others?
  • Are outcomes (of the meeting) safe to the planet?

Ecology check has been discussed in Chapter 2 (Section 2.4.1). The Cartesian coordinate has been illustrated with example. Through ecological frame, we wish to have congruence.

5.5   Discussion Using Six Thinking Hats

As discussed in Chapter 4 (Section 4.4), the leader or the facilitator will have a strategy on the sequence of using different hats. The meeting takes place using the plan. We can illustrate this with IT department's meetings on IT strategy. A chief information officer (CIO) asked three IT vice-presidents to prepare strategy proposal. He called a meeting to evaluate the strategies and finalise the overall IT strategy. This would have been a day-long discussion because of arguments and counter arguments. However, six thinking hats provide disciplined outcome-focused approach. Meetings are planned with the following strategies:

– Each strategy proposal

  • White hat 15 minutes—to cover all information about strategy and resources required for the execution of the strategy
  • Yellow hat 5 minutes—to show how the strategy fits in within the business
  • Black hat 5 minutes—to find the reasons for which the strategy will get rejected
  • Red hat 5 minutes—to understand what the gut feelings and expected emotional reactions are
  • Green hat 7.5 minutes—to generate ideas on how to overcome the constraints (black hat output) and strengthen the positive outcomes (yellow hat)
  • Blue hat 7.5 minutes—to summarise the findings for the strategy

– Consolidation to IT strategy

  • White hat 15 minutes—consolidated strategy presentation
  • Yellow hat 5 minutes—business alignments
  • Blue hat 5 minutes —summarise final proposed strategy

A good IT strategy plan can be developed and agreed within three hours. This is possible because of disciplined approach of six thinking hats.

5.6   Robert's Rule of Order for Meetings

Robert's Rules of Order (colloquially called Robert's rulebook) gives the procedure on how to conduct a formal meeting. It also gives a parliamentary process. The typical meeting is conducted with an agenda.

- Reading and approving the minutes of a meeting (MOM) of the previous meeting
- Presentation of reports—by officer, board, and standing committee
- Reports of special (select or ad hoc) committees
- Special orders
- Unfinished business and general orders
- New business

Robert rulebook gives a process of handling motion.

- A member seeks recognition for the floor.
- Chairman recognises the member (member obtains the floor).
- Member makes a motion.
- Another member seconds the motion.
- Chairman states the question.
- Debate (amendment and secondary motions).
- Chairman puts the question to vote.
- Chairman announces the result of the voting.

Many professional associations and societies use Robert's rules of order for the meetings. The meeting will have the role of a parliamentarian to ensure a smooth meeting using Robert's rules of order.

5.7   Impromptu Presentation

During the meeting, the participants should be ready to give impromptu presentation. Mark Twain once said, 'It usually takes me two or three days to prepare an impromptu speech.' In case of a meeting, if you are well prepared, impromptu presentation is not difficult. Some of the ways for impromptu presentation are listed below:

PREP (Point, Reason, Example, Point)

Meeting participants will state the *point* that he or she wants to make. He or she will give reasons to support his or her point and then will provide examples and elaborations. Finally, meeting participants will conclude with emphasising the point.

PIN (Positive, Interesting, Negative)

Edward de Bono suggests this technique to express without value judgement (truly unbiased). First, meeting participants tell the positives about the idea (or proposal). Next, they tell something interesting about the idea (or proposal). Finally, they mention something negative about the idea (or proposal).

5.8   Habits of Effective People

A meeting is a place where interdependence (Stephen Covey's concept in book '*The 7 Habits of Highly Effective People*') can be experienced. Habit 4 (think win-win), habit 5 (seek first to understand and then to be understood), and habit 6 (synergise) are practised.

'Think win-win' requires balanced approach (I am OK, you are OK), trusted relationship, and performance or partnership agreement. This is supported by systems and processes. This habit 4 brings mutually beneficial outcome. All elements of 'think win-win' are necessary for successful and effective meetings.

Essence of habit 5 is empathetic listening and clear communication. This is needed for the meetings.

Habit 6, 'synergise', is discussed in Chapter 3. This habit is to leverage individual talents to create whole output greater than sum of the individual's output.

5.9   Thinking Skills

John C. Maxwell classified thinking types into ten categories in his book *How Successful People Think*. Information processing is essentially thinking of participants and achieving meeting objectives. We can explore each category with a meeting.

- Shared thinking: A meeting is a shared thinking. Participants share their thinking in a cooperative mode.
- Big picture thinking: This is useful to understand the connection with a larger system and fitting your piece of work perfectly in a big picture.

- Focused thinking: This is useful for problem solving as we identify problem area, and focused thinking will give the root cause.
- Creative thinking: This is essential for idea generation and innovative solutions. Brainstorming meetings or green hat thinking sessions go with creative thinking.
- Realistic thinking: This is useful for fruition of dream. The reality thinking shows the gap between current state and goal achievement.
- Strategic thinking: This is required for long-term goals, vision, and mission. However, we have discussed (in Chapter 4) that strategy is a part of every change we plan and implement.
- Possibility thinking: This is required for converting idea into feasible solution and gives ability to make it happen.
- Reflective thinking: This is to get the learning points from experience (success as well as failures). This is necessary for post-project review and for continual improvements.
- Question popular thinking: This is necessary when we wish to step out of comfort zone. This will be useful in implementing a change.
- Unselfish thinking: This is necessary for win-win and useful for social responsibility.
- Bottom-line thinking: This is useful for assessment of situation and can be part of ecology check.

Participants should develop thinking skills and can choose necessary type of thinking. These are means to achieve the outcomes of meetings.

5.10 Decision-Making

Effectiveness of a meeting depends on brilliant decision-making and coming up with solid actions. Participants will have decision-making strategy (Chapter 4). When we could match their strategy, decision would be made quickly.

Another meta programme that plays a role in decision is convincer strategy. People have different ways as given below:

- Automatic—the decision is quick
- Number of times—need some time for number of experiences or reference

- Period of time—takes time to make acceptance
- Consistency—make sure about reliability and then make a decision

Subsequent sections give more ways to arrive at a decision. The unanimous decision or decision with consensus will be more acceptable than decision by voting. Hence, it is good to work on consensus in spite of longer time taken to reach consensus.

5.11   Reaching Consensus

Group meetings are not just discussion; we need to make a decision. Participants with diverse areas will have different concerns and opinions. The facilitator will have challenges to have consensus. Consensus does not mean compromise or unanimity. It is the solution that sufficiently addresses everyone's concerns or a better option among all options.

The facilitator can use the following guidelines:

- Confirm meeting objective: The meeting facilitator will state the resolution of the problem or issue or selection of the proposal or plan (Section 5.2).
- Agree on meeting plan/process: This is a part of meeting preparation (Chapter 4). However, the facilitator makes the participants aware of the process (Section 5.2).
- Presentation of ideas: This gives an opportunity for the participants to present their ideas, pros and cons.
- Identify area of agreement, disagreement, and priorities: Participants may find some aspects acceptable; those areas form an area of agreement. Participants will have concerns, and those areas form an area for disagreement. Participants can set the priorities.
- Resolve concerns: Participants look into alternatives and modifications so that majority of concerns are resolved.
- When majority of concerns are resolved, participants reach consensus.

Rapport and chunk-up/chunk-down/chunk lateral will help in conducting the discussion smoothly and reach consensus early.

5.12   Decision Making Using Voting

Sometimes we do not arrive at consensus or do not make decision unanimously; we can go for voting to make a decision.

We conduct voting to choose popular option or popular decision. General Henry Martin Robert gave a guiding principle, 'All shall be heard, but the majority shall decide'.

Three ways of voting are majority voting, multi-voting, and nominal group technique.

Majority voting

After the discussion, meeting participants will vote. Simple majority means more than 50 per cent vote. If constitution or rules state 2/3 majority or ¾ majority, then decision will be based on achieving required majority.

Multi-voting

After a discussion on options, options are numbered. Meeting participants will vote for option(s). If there are ten options, every participant will select three best solutions (one third options). The facilitator will tally the votes. Solution with least votes will be eliminated. Next round of voting is done, and options are further eliminated. Multiple round of voting is done till the best option is finalised.

Nominal group technique

After a discussion on options, numerical scale is decided. For example, scale 1 to 5 with 5 as the best and 1 as the least. Meeting participants will rate all the options. The facilitator will collect the voting slip and tally the rating for each option. Options with low total ratings will be dropped. The process is repeated till single best choice is found.

5.13   Conditional Close

In case of sales meetings, when a customer has an objection, the salesperson will use conditional close to move ahead with sales. Its format is 'If I could X, would you Y?' For example, if we could suggest you options for financing, will you buy now? (It is not 'Would you Y if I could X?' For example, will you buy now if we could suggest financing option?.)

Conditional close gives an alternative to objection and moves customer towards the sales transaction close. Condition close helps to move towards decision and towards achieving the purpose of the meeting.

5.14 In Summary

Participants can practise different skills and habits during the meeting. Observation skills (sensory acuity), thinking skills, questioning skills, facilitating skills, communication skills, presentation skills, and negotiation skills are some of the skills required during the meetings.

Meeting dynamics happens with active interaction among the participants and the tools used (some of the tools are shown in Figure 5.6).

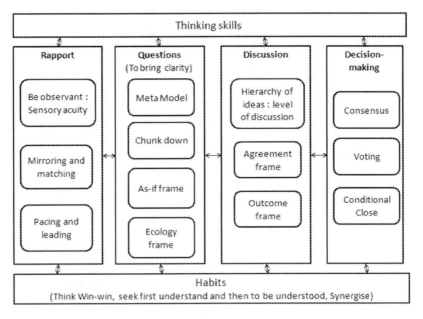

Figure 5.6: Interaction among different tools.

Rapport building is important for trusted environment of the meeting.

Questioning is key to bring clarity and black hat thinking.

The facilitator can use agreement frame and outcome frame during the discussion and decision-making and move towards the purpose of the meeting.

In case of a system, we looked at the tools like different cues for recognising representational system, tools for rapport building, tools for raising questions, and tools for decision-making.

In case of strategies, we used chunk-up to realise the common purpose and have a win-win. Another strategy is to focus on decision, using consensus and conditional closing.

Synergy is possible when we have a win-win attitude and empathy for each other.

5.15 Afterthought

After going through this chapter, you will have thoughts about the discussion in this chapter. Our theme is to build the systems, strategies and synergies for the meetings. With due respect to your model of the world, please jot down your thoughts on systems, strategies and synergies.

- What are the systems needed for a meeting?

_____

_____

_____

- What are the strategies required for a meeting?

_____

_____

_____

- How are the synergies built for a meeting?

_____

_____

_____

MEETING GAME RESULT: WIN-WIN

6. How Do I Conclude the Meeting and Do the Follow-Up?

Henry Wadsworth Longfellow says, 'Great is the art of beginning, but greater is the art of ending.' A facilitator has the responsibility to end the meeting on time with conclusion.

At the end of a sports event, there are results, winning on merit, lots of learning, and actions required for future. Major achievement is the fun enjoyed by all. In case of a meeting, the results are decisions made and tasks to be performed. Major achievement is participants' enjoyment and elevated energy levels.

This chapter gives important points in concluding a meeting and how to ensure the tasks decided in the meeting will be completed.

6.1   Summarising a Meeting

This will highlight the key discussion points, decisions, and action points. This will be the last chance for a facilitator or a leader to persuade and motivate the participants. Repetition of points is useful for reinforcing.

A facilitator or a leader can refer back to the opening of a meeting and check what has been achieved. If an agenda is incomplete due to time constraint or other reasons, the facilitator can schedule another meeting instead of dragging the meeting.

If there are incomplete tasks or task in progress, those tasks will be highlighted with the task owner. This will motivate to move forward.

Summarising will use backtrack frame and refrain from bringing new points.

In case six thinking hat methodology, blue hat thinking takes care of summarising and concluding a meeting

6.2   Backtrack Frame

At the time of conclusion, it is important that all participants are on the same page. This may not happen because of different filters acting in the participants' mind (refer Appendix A).

Backtrack frame is used to check agreements and understanding of participants. This is done by reviewing the meeting proceeding through the following:

- Using keywords
- Tonality of participants who presented the information

In case of a day-long meeting, backtrack framework is used for session conclusion. Session conclusion helps agreement framework.

6.3   Express Appreciation

A facilitator/leader must thank the participants for their time, participation, and contribution. Praise in public is a great motivator. The leader has the responsibility to end the meeting on high note and give energy to address action items.

Praise for good deeds deserves immediate appreciation or feedback. The leader should not delay appreciation and should motivate participants for their action.

6.4   Meeting Measurement

As mentioned in Chapter 1, what gets measured gets managed. Meetings should have measures to indicate performance. The performance can be evaluated based on the process and based on the roles performed by the participants.

Evaluation can be done by rating the activity and performance of role takers or by getting the comments on activity and performance. Rating will give general feedback, whereas comments will provide specific feedback. Rating could be 1 to 5 (1—strongly disagree, 2—disagree, 3—neutral/can't say, 4—agree, 5—strongly agree). The organisation can use the rating as per their standards on the feedback. Some organisations avoid the option 'neutral' so that the participants are forced to choose either 'agree' or 'disagree'.

Obtaining feedback

Meeting facilitator can allocate some time for meeting evaluation and feedback. Now a days, web-based survey tools are available. Participants can enter the data online, and the facilitator can generate report from the data in the system.

Feedback questions

Rating can be on the following generic questions:

- Purpose of the meeting was clear and positive.
- Meeting had right participants.
- Meeting facility was appropriate.
- Meeting agenda and document were provided adequately early.
- Meeting participants were well prepared.
- Meeting followed ground rules.
- Meeting pace was right, and time was well utilised (meeting efficiency).
- Meeting focused on purpose and was conducted as per agenda.
- Meeting participation was balanced; discussion was fruitful and led to a decision (meeting effectiveness).
- Meeting achieved the desired outcome, satisfying the purpose.
- Meeting could observe synergy among the participants.
- Meeting gave motivation, energy, and entertainment/enjoyment (energetic meeting).

Specific purposes like sales meetings and project meetings can add on questions related to those activities. If participants rate activity at 1 (strongly disagree), then the participants must give comments to justify the rating. In addition, comments can be asked for the following:

- Good practices in a meeting
- Improvements required

Other evaluation can be on the roles performed by the facilitator, presenter, timer, note taker, and participant. These can also have rating 1 to 5 (1—highly inadequate, 2—inadequate, 3—adequate, 4—good, 5—excellent). Generic questions can be the following:

- How well performed?
- Overall contribution?
- Helpful and supportive?

This will be the feedback to a specific person for his or her improvement.

The measurement should be linked to the performance indicators. Further performance indicator can form the balanced scorecard (refer to Chapter 10, Section 10.3).

6.5   Meeting Records

Minutes of a meeting (MoM) are the records of a meeting. Some meetings are as per the legislation (company law) or as per the management decision (for example, management review takes place every month). Minutes of meetings are for the compliance purpose.

Organisations will have a format for minutes of meeting. It should be used so that consistency is maintained. Some of the information will be similar to the agenda. Typical format will have following information:

- Date of the meeting
- Time of the meeting: In case of global meeting, mention clearly the time, for example, Pacific Standard Time (PST), Indian standard time (IST), and so on.
- Place of the meeting: In case of virtual meetings, place can be recorded against participants.
- Participants: (and as per requirement mention their department, organisation or place) Participants attended the meeting. Some organisations record absentees also.
- Record the discussion, decisions, acceptance and approvals. (Some processes require approval records; thus, acceptance is

decided during the meeting and approval is obtained separately through email or through system [like ERP system].)

• Action item, action by whom, and target date for completion.

Note taker will share a draft with the facilitator or leader and obtains approval. Then minutes of the meeting are circulated to all the participants, including those who were absent.

Note taker should be attentive to the details during the meeting and should prepare and circulate minutes as soon as possible. As time lapses, participants may forget about the meeting proceedings, timely minutes of the meeting will enforce the participants to take timely actions.

Book—Robert's rules of order is a good reference on recording meeting proceeding and preparing minutes of the meeting.

6.6 Follow-Up

Action items or tasks are the key output of a discussion and decisions during a meeting. Success of a meeting will depend on the actions taken. These actions need to be tracked through its status till it is closed. Only one participant will be made responsible for each action item to ease the tracking. He or she can delegate and tap the required resources.

Follow-up is often seen as just checking the status. In some organisations, we can see a long list of outstanding action items in the minutes of the meeting. This is a result of routine meetings, routine follow-ups, and routine delays.

Follow-up should go beyond status check; it should check the resource constraints and motivation of people working on the tasks.

It is useful to use outcome frame and evidence frame, which is discussed in the subsequent section. In addition, we are discussing prime concern and law of attraction.

As shown in Figure 6.1, during the meeting, only plans (construction in mind) are made; execution of those plans will realise the success for the organisation.

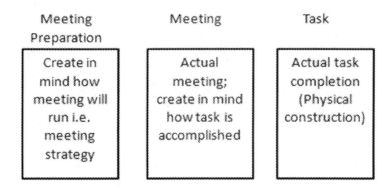

Figure 6.1: Begin with the end in mind.

A leader should consider the follow-up as an important activity for fruition of ideas. Complexity of follow-up depends on the organisation structure.

If organisation hierarchy is flat, meetings can involve different levels, and concept to implementation can be faster with easy follow-up.

If organisation hierarchy is tall, meetings will happen at various levels, which need time for understanding and approving. Thus, follow-ups become complex.

6.7   Outcome Frame

During the meeting, a leader should get commitment from the participants. The purpose of the meeting will be achieved when the tasks or action items are completed.

To ensure completion of a task or achieve desired outcome, the task should be expressed in SMART way.

- **S**pecific and **s**imple: The task defined in a specific and simple manner is easy to remember, and thus the mind will remain focused on it. If a meeting decides to increase sales by 10 per cent, the task should be 'achieve sales of N in region R for product P by second quarter ending in June 2013'. It is specific about the number to be achieved and also where, when, and which product. If the task is defined in a detailed manner, 'Get order of D from customer A, . . . customer B . . . customer Z.' Task definition will not be simple and will lose focus.

- **M**easurable and meaningful to you: There should be an evidence for achieving the task. Evidence frame is useful. In earlier example, sale is measurable in dollars. Tasks should be 'meaningful to you', that is, do you have passion for it? What is the motivation level?
- **A**ttainable and **as** if now: In above example, the required capabilities or the required potential is available for achieving the sale. *As if* now means the task is not expressed in future tense. If it is expressed in future tense, mind will tell that we have time for doing the task. Like tomorrow never comes, task will not be complete. Hence, *as if* now means the task is defined in present tense.
- **R**ealistic and **r**esponsible: This will look at the reality check. Sales team has the potential to get the order increase. However, if the production cannot produce additional 10 per cent, the sales team can get the orders, but those orders will not be fulfilled. This is to look at limiting factors. Responsibility means ownership. If sales manager delegates the task to the sales team, the sales manager cannot excuse for responsibility. The sales manager's responsibility remains with him, and he is also responsible for communicating the task to the sales team.
- **T**ime-bound and **t**owards what you want: Tasks must have expected date of completion. In the example, the date is given. Tasks should be expressed in a positive manner. Positive nature of meeting purpose is discussed in Chapter 2. It is applicable to tasks also. If sales task is stated as 'To obtain at least 1/3 of the total sale from region R', this will not work because of ambiguous definition with negative term *at least*.

With SMART definition, unconscious mind starts working, and accomplishment of task will be more certain.

6.8 Evidence Frame

This frame is linked to the outcome frame. It is related to monitoring the progress on achieving the outcome. As per NLP communication model, we get inputs through all five senses. We can ask the expected experience of all the senses.

- When you achieve the outcome, what will you see?
- When you achieve the outcome, what will you hear?
- When you achieve the outcome, what will you feel?
- When you achieve the outcome, what will you taste?
- When you achieve the outcome, what will you smell?

When a meeting participant is responsible for an action item, he or she thinks the outcome with all the senses in a positive way and the unconscious mind also works on it. He or she will work towards it with high energy and accomplish it.

6.9   Prime Concern: Starting, Changing, and Stopping

The conclusion of a meeting has action items for the participants. The action items need an initiation (starting of an action), performing (doing/making the change effective), and closing (completing the action). People will have preference or liking for one of these activities. The prime concern exercise can be performed by NLP master practitioner as this is covered at master practitioner level.

The prime concern concept has two questions:

- What are you best at—starting things, changing things, or stopping things?
- What are you worst at—starting things, changing things, or stopping things?

Meeting participants or team members will choose one of the three. Next question will be based on the response from the above questions.

- Worst at starting things, that is, trouble in being who they want to be: Is it that you are not being that you want to be?
- Worst at changing things, that is, trouble in doing what they want to do: Is it that you are not doing that you want to do?
- Worst at stopping things, that is, trouble in having what they want: Is it that you are not having that you want to have?

Third question will provide the prime concern, and this may be a stumbling block for completing the action items.

Meeting participant has informed his (or her) best option. We can ask the meeting participant or team member to remember the time when he (or she) was at his (or her) best.

Fourth and fifth questions will be the following:

- As you remember the time when you were at your best, what was present in that state that is not usually present?
- What was missing that is usually present in the normal routine awake state?

Answer to the fourth question will give the states at the best, for example, confident, brilliant, passionate, and so on, mentioned by the meeting participant.

Answer to the fifth question will give the missing states in routine, for example, confident, passionate, respected, and so on, mentioned by the meeting participants.

Combining the list of states will provide the resourceful states required to overcome the prime concern.

This whole exercise will provide the prime concern as well as the resources for doing the best that can address the prime concern.

6.10 Law of Attraction

As we talked about the energy level of the participants, let us also discuss about universal energy, especially law of attraction. In the novel *Alchemist* by Paulo Coelho, the core theme is 'when you want something, the entire universe conspires in helping you to achieve it'.

The Secret, the popular film and the book, gives details on the law of attraction. The core theme is, when you ask and believe, the power of universe takes care and you receive what you want. Three steps in the law of attraction are as given below:

- Ask: We need to think what we want. We need to visualise. We have already seen in evidence frame (what will you see).

- Believe: We need to believe that the law of attraction works and have a positive attitude. Our positive attitude and positive thinking attract positive things.
- Receive: When we express our want (step 1), we need not think how the want will be fulfilled. That will soon be apparent. We need to take an action, and the want will be fulfilled.

There is a criticism as well as an acceptance for the law of attraction. However, the following points are useful from tasks point of view:

- Visualisation has been considered as an important source for creativity. Meeting participants can use it for the task.
- Beliefs play an important role in accomplishing the task. The cycle of generative success starts with having a belief, then tapping the potential, then taking action, and finally achieving the result. In other words, if we believe that the task cannot be achieved, it will never be completed or never be done properly. When we have strong belief in completion of the task, we will draw our potentials and act on the task to achieve the outcome.
- Unconscious mind and intuition can provide different solution from the logical way of doing the task. Taking advantage of intuition is useful.

Some will have the tendency to think what they do not want. In such a case, write the contrast (do not want) and convert them into a positive statement. As per the law of attraction, the negative statement will attract the negative. It is important to ask in a positive manner.

6.11 In Summary

All is well that ends well. If a meeting is concluded with a high note and action items are completed, the meeting is very successful. Figure 6.2 shows the overall conclusion and follow-up.

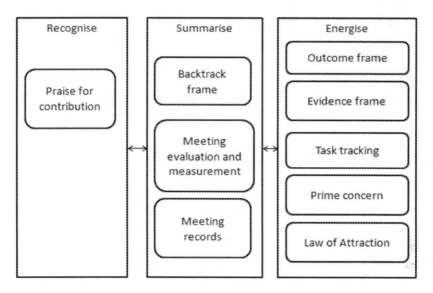

Figure 6.2: Concluding and follow-up.

Meetings set the direction for the task. An actual task or physical construction happens after the meeting. Tasks are expressed like SMART goal setting, and evidence frame is used to check its completion.

In the case of a system, we looked at the tools like backtrack frame, meeting evaluation, outcome frame, and evidence frame in concluding a meeting.

Our strategy is to energise the participants for the task completion and achievement of the meeting purpose.

6.12 Afterthought

After going through this chapter, you will have thoughts about the discussion in this chapter. Our theme is to build the systems, strategies and synergies for the meetings. With due respect to your model of the world, please jot down your thoughts on systems, strategies and synergies.

- What are the systems needed for a meeting?

- What are the strategies required for a meeting?

_____

_____

_____

- How are the synergies built for a meeting?

_____

_____

_____

MEETING GAME:

PROBLEMS AND CONFLICTS

7. Meetings for Problem Solving

Harlan Cleveland, a US diplomat and scholar, once quoted, 'Leaders are problem solvers by talent and temperament, and by choice.' Leaders often conduct meetings for problem solving. They get the pool of people with diverse experience and knowledge. The meetings are conducted to derive the best solution. Leaders will use brainstorming meetings for creative solution to a problem as well as creative solution for future plans.

In the sports event, it may be possible that conflicts or problems arise within a team, or there may be a conflict with the teams. This is not a healthy sign. It may affect the team's performance. Sports team leader will work on resolution. Similarly, meetings will have certain issues; they can be resolved through planned steps and by using tools.

This chapter will look at two key meeting types—problem-solving meetings and brainstorming meeting, Some of the tools used in these meetings have been discussed. In addition, conflict resolution is discussed.

7.1   Problem-solving Meetings

Problem-solving meetings are called to find the solutions to the problems through group thinking. These meetings can have four steps:

- confirming the problem or discussion objective(Refer Chapter 2),
- identifying major causes (Refer section 7.2),
- identifying potential solution (Refer section 7.4), and
- making a decision (Refer sections 5.10 to 5.13).

In case of problem solving, the key step is to find the cause of the problem, especially the root cause. We can resolve the problem by addressing the root cause. Cause and effect analysis is very helpful in finding the root cause and providing the good problem solution.

When we do not have proper analysis, then we could get superficial answers. For example,

- What is the chief cause of failures among the students? Exams are the chief cause of failures.
- What is the chief cause of divorce? Marriage is the chief cause of divorce.

Let us see what can be done for effective cause and effect analysis. We look at some techniques—fishbone diagram, fault tree analysis, failure mode effect and criticality analysis, and Kepner Treoge model.

7.2   Problem-solving Tools

Fishbone diagram:

This is also known as cause and effect diagram or Ishikawa diagram. Generic diagram for manufacturing scenario is shown in Figure 7.1. In a fishbone diagram, effect or problem is shown on the right-hand side box, and all possible causes are shown as the branches. Causes will have groups and subgroups. An analysis brings in comprehensive list of possible causes with clear classification. Further causes can be divided based on 80:20 rule, that is, 80 per cent of problem is due to 20 per cent causes. We can act on those 20 per cent causes to resolve the problem.

A leader can conduct a brainstorming session and explore the causes. Typical manufacturing scenario will look at 5Ms—*men* (people) involved in the work, *method* (process) used for manufacturing, *material* (inputs) used in production, *machines* (tools) used in production, and *measurements* (or checks) performed during production. Typical service scenario will look at the skills (of the people), suppliers (inputs), system (processes and tools) and surrounding (environment).

The limitation of fishbone diagram is, it does not show the sequence of events (cause) that leads to final event (effect)

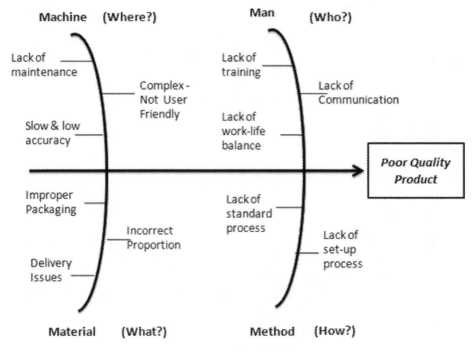

Figure 7.1: Fishbone diagram.

Fault Tree Analysis (FTA):

Fault tree analysis is another type of diagrammatic representation of the cause of failure. Figure 7.2 shows a simple fault tree. However, to find the root cause, the leader can conduct brainstorming session and explore the different failure paths in a fault tree. In case of a fault tree analysis, effect is shown at the top and causes are shown below. However, the causes are clubbed with AND gate or OR gate. AND gate means all causes below must happen together and OR gate means any one cause can trigger the event.

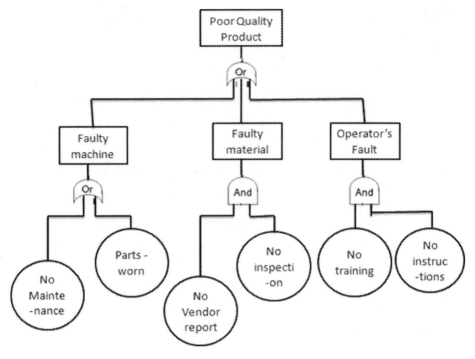

Figure 7.2: Fault tree analysis.

Fault tree analysis has a top-down approach. We need to find the events that have contributed to the top event. The lowest level events are the root causes.

Failure Mode Effect (and Criticality) Analysis (FEMA/FEMCA):

Failure mode effect analysis or failure mode effect and criticality analysis has bottom-up approach. Each component is analysed for its different modes of failure and its effect (on a product). Further, the criticality is assessed to gauge the risk which has two parameters— likelihood of failure and impact of failure. This method is meticulous as each component is analysed. Simple example is given in Table 7.1.

This technique is used during design stage so that product is designed for quality. This is problem prevention.

Component	Failure mode	Effect	Action
Operator	Not able to operate properly	Defective product	Training for operator or Provide step-by-step instructions
Material	Defective	Defective product	Inspect material Or Inspection report from vendor
Machine	Misalignment	Defective product	Maintenance as per schedule

Table 7.1: Failure mode effect analysis.

Kepner Treoge (KT) Model:

Kepner Treoge has developed a problem-solving and decision-making model. Key point in this model is detailed problem specification. Model suggests exploring 4 areas—problem identification (what), problem location (where), problem timing (when), and problem size (extent). It also brings more clarity by defining what 'the problem is' and what 'the problem is not'. Model does not focus on 'why' so that problem solving will not jump to false cause. The detailing brings all facts of problem and concludes with a root cause.

5 Why:

This is another way to find the root cause. In this method, we will question why the problem did occur and repeat it till the root cause is found. Generally, we can get the root cause with asking why five times. Hence, it is called '5 why' method. This is the opposite of KT model. NLP philosophy (Chapter 5, Section 5.4 discusses on using Meta model) does not support this technique because the question 'why' can lead to a divergent thinking and different participants will provide different reasons (or excuses). If this tool '5 why' is used in a meeting, the meeting facilitator needs to be careful about the assumptions, keeping the connection with original problem.

7.3   Cause and Effect: NLP Concept

This is not about finding the cause but about the responsibility for change or results. The question is, are we a part of the cause or the effect? For example, the operator in manufacturing environment is producing defective products. If he considers himself as a part of the effect, he will blame others for not giving training or for not doing maintenance. In short, the operator is having only one option to wait for others to take action. If the operator considers himself as a part of the cause, he takes the responsibility for the situation that has created the defective product. He explores the cause and takes responsibility for corrective action. He will take initiative for training, material inspection or machine maintenance.

7.4   Brainstorming Meetings

Brainstorming meetings are used for idea generation. In case of six thinking hats, it is green hat thinking. This gives an opportunity for creative thinking. Edward de Bono suggests using lateral thinking to become more creative and productive during the green hat thinking. The leader should create a mood of excitement about the session and choose the venue where creativity is reflected (for example, wall is a whiteboard). Important principles are the following:

- No idea is rejected. Wild ideas are also accepted. All ideas are listed and displayed.
- Meeting participants may develop ideas on each other's ideas.
- Meetings look for quantity and not quality; hence, discussion, analysis, or judgement is not allowed.

There can be a separate meeting for analysis of ideas. Analysis can start with affinity analysis to put similar ideas under one category. Post-it notes may be used to write ideas. This helps to display the ideas and ideas can be easily moved while forming different categories.

Duplicate ideas and irrelevant ideas can be eliminated. Then best solution can be selected through decision making process (sections 5.10 to 5.12). However, it is a good practice to have an inventory of ideas than discarding the rejected ideas. The rejected ideas will also be available in the future.

The facilitator can conduct a session in a fashion that encourages creativity. Some of ways are listed below:

- Round Robin brainstorming: Participants will give ideas as per their turn in a circle. The advantage is that each participant gets an opportunity to speak. If a participant does not have an idea, then the participant will say pass to the next participant. When all participants say pass, no more new ideas are available and the session can come to an end.
- Paper and pencil brainstorming: Participants will write the ideas on a paper and then share them. Participants can choose to remain anonymous by not writing the name on the paper.
- Free-form brainstorming: Anyone can suggest an idea as it is popped up in the participants' mind. The disadvantage is some participants may remain quiet.

7.5 Tools for Brainstorming

Mind Map (Or Spidergram):

This is a graphical representation of ideas generated. Instead of making a list, mind map is similar to the way the mind works, that, branching and spreading. This is also called radiant thinking. Brainstorming can use this tool. Brainstorming using mind map can utilise colours, symbols, and pictures for creative imagination. Figure 7.3 shows this example. The aim or purpose is written at the centre node, and supporting ideas are shown around. We can further expand similar ideas or related ideas on the same branch.

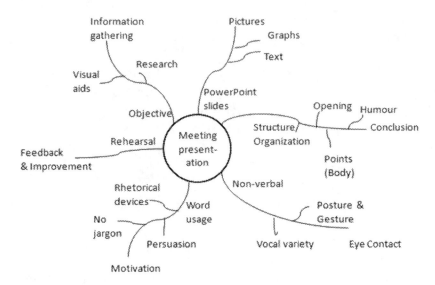

Figure 7.3: Mind map for the preparation of meeting presentation.

Use of random words:

Unrelated words selected randomly can stimulate creativity and develop ideas. We can use a dictionary, a book, or a magazine for random word selection.

SCAMPER technique

This is useful for brainstorming for a new product or service or for improving the existing one. Mnemonic SCAMPER stands for the following:

- Substitute: In case of a product, can we substitute with lighter material (weight reduction)/cheaper material (cost reduction) without sacrificing on quality? In case of a process, can we substitute the process step (e.g. 100 per cent inspection by sampling inspection)?
- Combine: Can we have casting of one single piece (combined) instead of welding three parts?
- Adapt: Can we adapt industrial waste in a recycling process?
- Modify: Can we modify this process/device to utilise in a new process?

- Put to another use: Can we use this raw material in a new product?
- Eliminate: Can we eliminate a step from the process?
- Reverse/rearrange: Can we rearrange steps for faster results?

We can think of a question based on SCAMPER and come up with innovative product, service, or process.

7.6   Imagination and Visualisation

NLP communication model (refer Appendix A) shows that our experience is stored in all sensory forms, that is, visual, auditory, kinaesthetic, olfactory, and gustatory. Our mind does not distinguish between real and imaginary. We can experience through imagination. We can engage all five senses to fuel our creativity and holistic perspective. Albert Einstein said, 'Imagination is more important than knowledge. For knowledge is limited to all we know and understand, while imagination embraces the entire world and all there ever will be to know and understand.'

The word *imagination* is derived from an image, that is, a picture. Visualisation of a picture is an important part of imagination. We often tend to underrate ourselves for our visualisation capacity. However, our brain is equipped for imagination; we need to use our brain, practise visualisation, and tap our creative capabilities.

Imagination is useful for brainstorming as well as problem solving.

7.7   Conflict Resolution

When participants (two or more) have unresolved differences, real or perceived, they are in conflict. Conflict may arise in a meeting or a leader needs to have the meeting for conflict resolution. Reasons for conflict may be the following:

- Misunderstanding: Misunderstanding can happen due to perception or miscommunication. Prevention of this cause can be through rapport (refer Chapter 5), respect to different opinion, and recognition of their model of the world (refer Appendix B).

- Working style: People have different working style (e.g. dominator/authoritarian or harmoniser/democratic). Mismatch of working style can lead to a conflict. Prevention of this cause can be through understanding people and their behaviour (refer Chapter 3).
- Issues: Team members will have different preferences over the work methods, though they have the same mission. These issues can lead to a conflict. Prevention of this cause can be through the neurological levels and clarity at each level (refer Chapter 2).
- Contentious personalities: It may be difficult to work with some personalities like 'know it all', an argumentative person, and so on. Prevention of this cause can be through understanding people and their behaviour (refer Chapter 3).

There are five options for resolving a conflict:

- Turtle strategy: This is to avoid a conflict by withdrawing. There are no winners or no losers. This is not a good option as it is postponing the conflict than a real resolution.
- Shark strategy: This is to compete and use power to win. There is 'I win; you lose'. This is not a good option as a loser can retaliate.
- Teddy bear strategy: This is to accommodate and appease others by downplaying. This is 'I lose; you win'. This is not a good option as people may lose credibility.
- Fox strategy: This is to compromise and derive equality by losing something to gain something. This is 'I bend; you bend'. This is not a good option as this may lead to derailment of long-term plan.
- Owl strategy: This is to collaborate and work through the differences. This will lead to creative solutions that will satisfy both. This is a win-win situation and most desired option.

Facilitating collaboration

From meeting perspective, the important task is how to facilitate the collaboration and resolve conflict. The following guidelines (same as Section 5.9) are useful:

- Have open communication and allow all the parties to speak. Rapport (refer Chapter 5.3) and detailed discussion (Chapter 5) are important in an open communication.

- Encourage all the parties to listen.
- Identify the areas of agreement. Build agreement frame and use chunk-up (Chapter 5).
- Identify the areas of disagreement. Use chunk-up and chunk-down (Chapter 5).
- Search for solution.
- Reach consensus.

7.8   Perceptual Positions

Perceptual positions technique is a concept to understand other person's perspective and viewing an event from neutral person's perspective. This may be handy in resolving a conflict. Facilitator can use perceptual positions prior to the conflict resolution meeting. He (or she) should be an NLP practitioner to conduct the session. He (or she) will ask a person to recollect the scenario when the conflict surfaced. He (or she) will mark three positions. As per the scenario, person will stand or sit for the first and second positions. Figure 7.4 shows first and second positions as standing and third position should be able to view those two positions independently. Those three positions and thought process are as follows:

- First position (own shoe/our own map of the world)

  - How are you behaving and feeling?
  - What is important to you? What do you want?
  - What is there to learn? What are the changes to your perception?

- Second position (their shoe/their map of the world). Now experience the scenario from their point and answer the same questions:

  - How are you behaving and feeling?
  - What is important to you? What do you want?
  - What is there to learn? What are the changes to your perception?

- Third position (observer). Imagine yourself as a butterfly on the wall and experience the scenario again and answer the following questions:

  - How each of them is behaving and feeling?

- • What is important to each of them?
- • What is there to learn? What are the changes to your perception?

– Comeback to position 1 with all learning and perception.

– How would you like to resolve the conflict?

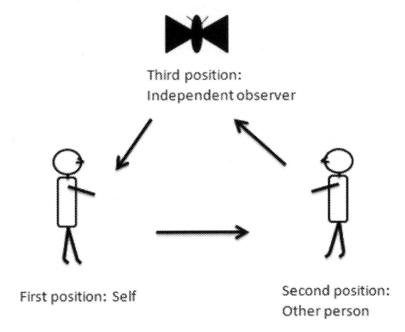

Third position:
Independent observer

First position: Self

Second position:
Other person

Figure 7.4 Perceptual positions

This exercise will resolve the conflict with better understanding of each other. This will encourage them to listen to each other and move towards the conflict resolution.

7.9   In Summary

Executives need to conduct meetings for problem-solving and idea-generation session. Effective use of the tools and visualisation ability will make meetings successful in resolving the issues.

In case of a system, we looked at the tools like cause-and-effect diagram, fault tree analysis, failure mode effect analysis, mind map, SCAMPER technique, and perceptual positions.

In case of strategies, we focus on being a part of the cause and take actions and we resolve a conflict with win-win.

7.10 Afterthought

After going through this chapter, you will have thoughts about the discussion in this chapter. Our theme is to build the systems, strategies and synergies for the meetings. With due respect to your model of the world, please jot down your thoughts on systems, strategies and synergies.

- What are the systems needed for a meeting?

_____

_____

_____

- What are the strategies required for a meeting?

_____

_____

_____

- How are the synergies built for a meeting?

_____

_____

_____

MEETING GAME: ROLES

8. Key Roles in a Meeting

Daiseku Ikeda, an educator, Buddhist philosopher, and peace-builder says, 'People always have many different roles to play. The crucial thing is to be determined to make a wholehearted effort in everything and be fully engaged in what we are doing at any given moment. The secret to successfully fulfilling a variety of roles is to concentrate fully on the task at hand and give it our best effort with enthusiasm, maintaining a positive, forward-looking attitude and not worrying.'

In sports events, there are different roles. In case of soccer, the referee needs to be neutral. In case of cricket, the tournament appoints neutral umpires. When the players are underperforming or the team is not performing, a coach can play an important role in uplifting the performance. In case of a meeting, the facilitator is neutral. Sometimes, a leader becomes the coach for the subordinates. They are crucial to successful meetings.

Meeting process has shown different roles (Chapters 1 and 4). However, this chapter selects three key roles to discuss the qualities required and NLP technique 'modelling' to learn from your role model.

8.1   Facilitator

Today's organisations use diverse technologies. Globalisation has brought together people from different parts of the world. Projects and operational works often engage people across different functional teams. A leader takes a challenge to coordinate the meetings for the projects and work with diversity in terms of people and technologies. In other terms, he or she needs to play a role of a facilitator. To become a good facilitator, we can consider the following qualities:

- Present an issue/problem/topic in concise and clear manner.
- Encourage participation in the discussion.
- Control the discussion.
- Manage time.

- Handle the challenging situation.
- Help the group to arrive at a decision.

8.2   Coach

A leader or a manager requires one-to-one meetings with the subordinates. He or she needs to guide subordinates on performance, career, or resolution of issues. In such meetings, the leader or the manager takes the role of a coach. To become a good coach, we can consider the following qualities:

- Listen actively.
- Establish rapport and build confidence.
- Encourage self-discovery.
- Praise positive results.

8.3   Negotiator

In many meetings, we work towards agreement with people through negotiations. Hence, we often play a role of a negotiator in the meeting. To become a good negotiator, we can consider following qualities:

- Work to achieve mutual success with win-win mindset.
- Have flexibility and non-dogmatic way to have multiple options.
- Visualise bigger picture and set high goals.
- Listen actively.
- Consider a part of team and work as a team player.
- Understand clearly what is needed and work with the plan.
- Be honest and direct.

8.4   Modelling: NLP Concept

When we think about sports or music, we often have idols, for example, Sachin Tendulkar in cricket, David Beckham in football, or Michael Jackson in music. The list can be never ending. We want to be like them. However, the question arises is, how we should model them. NLP has the answer.

In case of meetings, we can think on how we can become a good facilitator, a good coach, or a good negotiator. It may be possible that we may have role models for these meeting roles or we admire some of the facilitators of TV talk shows. NLP modelling shows how to learn from your role model.

Robert Dilt has illustrated the modelling aspects in depth in his book *Modelling with NLP*. We will explore a few aspects with reference to meetings.

The skills can be classified at six levels based on complexity:

- Simple behaviour skills: This is about gestures and posture that can be easily noticed. For example, in case of a meeting, the presenter shows centre stance, displaying confidence.
- Simple cognitive skills: This is easily identifiable mental process. For example, in a meeting, the participant or the presenter provides a definition of a term through remembrance or gives synonyms and explains (vocabulary skills).
- Simple linguistic skills: This is an ability to ask simple question so that it brings specificity. The comment is: 'Communication is missing.' The question on the comment is: 'Who has not communicated to whom? What has not been communicated?'
- Complex behavioural skills: This is a combination of simple behavioural skills. Presentation in a meeting is an example of this type of skill. Presentation will use variety of body language—gesture, postures, and stage movement that will enhance the presentation.
- Complex cognitive skills: This is a combination of simple thinking skills and synthesising. In a meeting, the summariser pulls the discussion points together and derives a conclusion. The initiator suggests an idea to resolve the problem in discussion.
- Complex linguistic skills: This is an interaction with people with influence, for example, persuading and negotiating. These language skills can challenge the limiting beliefs. For example, if someone comments, 'This problem can be solved by experienced person only', then the challenging question is 'Are creative ideas/ solutions coming only through experience?'

Another aspect of modelling is to look at skill dimensions. Robert Dilt has mentioned six skill dimensions. We can explore them from meeting perspective:

- Conceptual: We need to ask the purpose of possessing the skills of a facilitator/coaching skills/negotiation skills and when we will use those skills.
- Analysis: We need to find the difference that makes a difference, that is, the elements or distinctions for successful facilitation, coaching, or negotiation.
- Observation: This is for non-verbal communication for success and finding patterns.
- Following procedure: These are step-by-step process of facilitation/coaching/negotiation.
- Interacting with others: These are the responses to the responses/action by others. Facilitation, coaching, and negotiation are interactive processes.
- Managing relationship: This is the flexibility to respond as per variations in the pattern, for example, variation in facilitating a group at norming stage and a group at storming stage.

Modelling uses different tools. These tools are studied at advanced levels of NLP training. Some of them are as follows:

- TOTE (test operate test exit)
- BAGEL (body posture or breathing, accessing cues [non-verbal or anything else], gestures, eye movements, language patterns)
- ROLE (representational system—visual, auditory, kinaesthetic; orientation—external, remembered, constructed; links—sequential, simultaneous; effect—access, evaluate, input, organise)
- SOAR (state operator and results)
- SCORE (symptom, cause, outcome, resources, and effect)

The tools are used for different purposes. However, the generic steps of modelling are as follows:

- Select expert to model the skill.
- Analyse the elements.
- Consider physiology—non-verbal.

- Analyse strategies, motivation, and filters.
- Analyse contrast—drop unrelated elements and keep essential elements.
- Determine the critical elements.
- Install elements in self and test the results.
- Develop training programme.

8.5   In Summary

A leader or a participant(s) of a meeting takes the role of a facilitator, a coach, or a negotiator. We come across role models in these areas within the organisation or outside the organisation. NLP concept 'modelling' gives a detailed approach towards learning from the role models to become successful. It looks at skill level, skill dimensions, and steps to understand the essential elements of the skills.

In case of a system, we looked at the tools like modelling.

Our strategy is to look for the best and model him or her.

8.6 Afterthought

After going through this chapter, you will have thoughts about the discussion in the chapter. Our theme is to build the systems, strategies and synergies for the meetings. With due respect to your model of the world, please jot down your thoughts on systems, strategies and synergies.

- What are the systems needed for a meeting?

_____

_____

_____

- What are the strategies required for a meeting?

_____

_____

_____

- How are the synergies built for a meeting?

_____

_____

_____

MEETING GAME: FUN

9. Humour in a Meeting

Toastmasters Public Speaking World Champion (2001) Darren LaCroix says, 'When you humourise, you humanise.' Humour has its own importance in communication, and meetings are no exception. Humour has often been the key to unlock participation in the meeting. Some executives shy away from humour because they feel it may be undignified. However, the apt, well-timed humour in the opening of the meeting will immediately put the participants on high energy.

Fun is always a part of sports event. Fun will be off the field with spectators showing funny slogans and boards and on the field with some funny actions by players or funny celebration. Many times incidents are taken sportingly, and fun is enjoyed. In a meeting, fun and entertainment can play an important role.

We will look at the need for humour, humour bone in everyone, important questions to use humour, and NLP connection.

9.1   Need for Humour

To encourage the executives and the leaders to use humour, we can utilise David McClelland's motivation theory—Power, Affiliation and achievement with NLP perception filter 'away' and 'towards'.

- Power and control—away

  When a leader talks monotonously without any fun, participants' mind will wander and the leader will not get the required attention. Participants in a meeting may be preoccupied with different thoughts; a start without attention will result in loss of control.

- Power and control—towards

  If a leader gives humorous touch in the opening or gives a plan for fun and exciting meeting, the leader gets immediate attention.

It gives a power to make the meeting a pleasant exercise with the use of humour. Participants will attentively listen and enjoy their participation.

- Affiliation and popularity—away

If a leader has a serious face and serious talk, this may spread negativism. Participants would like to stay away. The leader will find it difficult to have camaraderie.

- Affiliation and popularity—towards

If a leader has a smile on his or her face and has an ability to add funny punchlines, the participants will giggle or laugh. The company that laughs together stays together. Humour makes a person user-friendly and acceptable. It makes a warm and healthy environment for the meeting and results in camaraderie.

- Achievement and success—away

When a leader gives stressful work and gives tensions on achieving targets, productivity decreases, creativity vanishes, and achievements slip. The leader will have more hurdles for success.

- Achievement and success—towards

When a leader is fun-loving, the fun becomes a stress reliever. Humour also has creativity aspects. It propels creativity among the participants. Stress-free and creative environment brings productivity boost. The leader can achieve success by exceeding the targets.

In short, humour helps in getting attention and listening. It acts as a lubricant for friendly environment and helps in creativity.

9.2 Sense of Humour

There is a need to understand a distinction between jokester's joke and humour by an executive. The choice of material differs. To get laughs, the jokester depends on one-liners and stories usually irrelevant to the event. The executive never loses the focus on the purpose of the meeting. Humour and the laughs generated are supportive to the points in the meeting. Humour narrows or eliminates the gulf among the participants, managers, and leaders.

Another way to analyse humour is transactional analysis and ego states (developed by US psychiatrist Eric Berne). Eric Berne talked about three ego states—parent, adult, and child in his transactional analysis concept.

Parent ego state represents behaviours and thoughts that are copied from our parents. Parent ego state has two types—one is critical parents, that is, being linked to discipline, limits and rules, and so on, and the second is nurturing parents, that is, being linked to protection, love, and so on. The dominator person in the meeting may have critical parent ego state.

Adult ego state is unemotional and linked to organising, decision-making, problem-solving, and so on. Executives in the meeting will operate through adult ego state.

Child ego state is linked to feelings and impulses that come naturally to the child. Child ego state is divided into four types—adapted child, rebellious child, natural child, and little professor.

Adapted child will be asking for permission, shows helplessness, and remains quiet. The withdrawer or sleeper (behaviour of individuals) in the meeting may have adapted child ego state.

Rebellious child is complaining, procrastinating, defiant, and so on. The destroyer, aggressor, or blocker in the meeting may have rebellious child ego state.

Free or natural child is playful and joyful. The playboy/girl in the meeting may have free child ego state.

Little professor is curious and creative. Little professor provides the quality required for the sense of humour. The tension reliever in the meeting may have little professor ego state.

The adult ego state and little professor ego state are useful ego states for the meeting.

A child laughs several times in a day as the little professor in a child (person) is more active. With the growth over the years, people will have less little professor ego state.

Executives can awaken his or her little professor and tune the funny bone. It is good to be alert about the sources of humour and record humorous story or anecdote quickly than relying on memory to retrieve. We can read jokes in newsletters, newspapers, and magazines. We can listen to a humorous talk show on radio and watch comedy shows on TV. Internet provides a number of sites for humour. The witty jesters of ancient time provide good stories for different situations. Aesop or Birbal and Tenali Raman from India have stories with management moral. It is a good practice to have a humour file as we cannot remember all the jokes and funny incidents.

Another source is your own experiences at various places—office, home, or in travel. An IT manager once said, 'I wish to start a stand-up meeting.' An IT analyst responded, 'But all the meeting rooms have chairs.' The team had giggles.

9.3   Humour Selection: Important Questions

An executive will select humour or a humorous story to emphasise his point. Good humour will not offend or hurt any person, group, or community. Hence, the executive should ask himself or herself, 'Would I feel comfortable saying it?' This should check whether humour has positive spirit.

The executive should ask, 'Is the one-liner or the story related to the business dealt in the meeting?' This will check the connection between the point to be illustrated and humour. The executive should use the punchline correctly and should not explain the connection. Participants will understand it as per their model of the world.

The executive should ask, 'Is it funny?' The story may appeal to some of the participants and some people may not respond with laughter or giggle. The executive should use his or her own judgement on humour level. It is good to say 'I wish to share a story' instead of 'I wish to share a joke'. Joke sets high expectation on fun part. When the story turns out to be funny, people enjoy it.

The executive should ask, 'Is it presentable?' The executive should develop presentation skill for humour. It may require vocal variety and presentation of the punchline in a right manner. If humorous story requires a lot of body language, it may not be presentable in the meeting.

We can also look at the questions suggested by Rick Segel and Darren LaCroix in their book *Laugh & Get Rich: How to Profit from Humor in Any Business*:

- How can you relieve your own tension?
- How can you relieve the tension of others?
- How can we make this fun?

We can look at the example of humour usage by a quality manager to appeal for process compliance. He used Birbal's story to illustrate the point. Story goes as follows:

Emperor Akbar received three identical statuettes from a neighbouring king, who had asked Emperor Akbar to rate them as good, better, and best. Courtier could not find the difference. Finally, it was Birbal's turn. Birbal observed the statuettes carefully. He found a small hole in the right ear. Birbal took a small metal piece and inserted it in the right ear. For the first statuette, it came out of the left ear. For the second statuette, it came out of the mouth, and for the third statuette, it became a part of statuette as it did not come out.

Birbal graded first statuette as good, second as better, and third as best. Akbar's courtiers could not understand the ratings. Then Birbal explained that statuettes were similar to people. First type listens and forgets. Second listens and talks about it but will not be doing it. Third type is 'say what they do; then do what they said'. Hence, these people are graded as the best.

The quality manager asked, 'May I know in which category you belong to?' The response was 'We are the best, and we show process compliance.'

NLP suggests using metaphor to move to a desired state. Use of humorous stories in a meeting can make the meetings interesting and also put across the intended message.

Participants would like to have excitements in the meeting. Routine meetings will be predictable, and this will lead to boredom. There is a need for creative solutions to make the meetings interesting.

A quality manager wanted to get ready for an external audit. He did not conduct internal audits or briefings. He designed games based on popular shows 'Jeopardy' and 'Who Wants to be a Millionaire?' Participants enjoyed the game and retained the points very well.

9.4   Humour Anchor

NLP has a term called *anchor*. Anchors are triggers or stimulus to a desired state (state of mind like cheerful, elated friendly, and so on.). These are memory pegs to connect the information stored in the brain. A leader can use humour as an anchor. This can be understood by an example.

An IT department had a meeting to review the performance indicators (statistics). IT teams used to measure mean time between failure (MTBF).

The IT manager said, 'There is a story of a statistician who asked for average depth of water and got drowned. MTBF is a good measure; however, I want to know the longest downtime suffered by our users.'

Drowned statistician became the anchor word to provide a meaningful statistics in the report and in the meeting.

9.5   Humour State

One of the NLP presuppositions is 'The mind and body are parts of the same system and affect each other'. (Refer Appendix A, NLP Communication Model, to understand the link among the state, physiology, and behaviour.) The state of mind is important for work to proceed. Negative states like sadness, rejection, and anger are not resourceful states and will result in a loss of productivity. If the meetings start with humour, participants will be in a humorous state, which frees stress and creates friendly environment.

Humour requires creativity, for example, humour through exaggeration or connecting two dissimilar things. Humour can lead to creative solution. Rick Segel gave his experience in the book *Laugh & Get Rich: How to Profit from Humor in Any Business*. Rick was responsible to find a convenient and economical space for New England Speaker's Association (NESA) meetings. Rick jokingly said, 'I guess we will just have to buy a building and rent out the space when we don't use it.'

Another member of NESA asked, 'Was that supposed to be funny?'

Rick replied, 'I am brainstorming. My best ideas came from the absurd.' The solution was to contact all the companies in the area that might have meeting space to rent out on a Saturday.

Another example is from an IT department. The accounts department implemented new accounting software, effective from the new financial year. Unfortunately, errors appeared in the first month's financial report due to software bugs. As the first month report was incorrect, year to date figures in subsequent months were also incorrect, and troublesome rework was necessary. Accounts department and IT departments had a meeting to resolve the problem.

The IT department was giving a solution of data correction. The accounts department was not agreeing due to lack of transaction traceability and question of data integrity. One person jokingly said, 'Ask Spielberg for time machine (movie *Back to the Future*) to correct the accounts.' An IT analyst seriously considered a very short downtime to run accounting computer program with past date and resolved the issue of incorrect year-to-date reports. This shows humour can give solution.

9.6   In Summary

Efficiency of a meeting is directly related to the state of mind. The dry content of a meeting will put the participants in an unproductive mode. There is a need for creative thinking to have fun in the meetings. The adult ego state works in a logical manner. It is good to have the little professor ego state to make the meetings interesting through humour. We can tap various resources for humour (books, newsletter, or own experience) and make a point to bring smile, giggle, and laughter in the meeting.

In case of a system, we looked at the tools like developing and recording humour file.

In case of strategy, it is to take full advantage of humour. For synergy, humourised meetings can synergise.

9.7   Afterthought

After going through this chapter, you will have thoughts about the discussion in this chapter. Our theme is to build the systems, strategies and synergies for the meetings. With due respect to your model of the world, please jot down your thoughts on systems, strategies and synergies.

- What are the systems needed for a meeting?

_____

_____

_____

What are the strategies required for a meeting?

_____

_____

_____

How are the synergies built for a meeting?

_____

_____

_____

TO THE NEXT MEETING GAME

10. Next Step

Meetings can become efficient, effective, and energetic. However, transformation will not happen overnight. This requires systematic planning for moving from current state to desired state.

In case of sports events, sports persons always look forward. He or she takes learning from the events, starts working on improvements in performance, and looks forward to the next event. In case of a meeting, the meeting participants and the organisation can work on improvements in the meetings.

Continual improvement is a part of today's businesses. Meeting process should monitor its improvement cycle. Meetings will have performance indicators. These can be monitored and used to verify improvements.

This chapter explores how assessment is done and how balanced scorecard is used for meetings.

10.1 Assessment and Goal Setting

We discussed process approach to the meetings in Chapter 1 and also considered process maturity as an indicator of implementation of process. Control objectives for information and related technology (COBIT) has defined six attributes for maturity. These attributes are useful for assessing the maturity of the process. (For details refer to COBIT. Lowest maturity level 1 and highest maturity level 5 are discussed here. The other levels are between these two levels.)

The maturity attributes are the following:

- Awareness and communication: At maturity level 1, communication on issues is sporadic. At maturity level 5, communication on issues is proactive. This attribute can be linked to the system, that is, communication channels or tools and strategy, that is, communication plan.

- Policies, plans, and procedures: At maturity level 1, process and practices are ad hoc. At maturity level 5, there are automated, integrated, and standardised processes of world class. Policies and plans are part of strategy, whereas procedures are a part of the system.
- Tools and automation: At maturity level 1, there is no planned approach for tool usage. At maturity level 5, there will be standard tools, improving the process. This attribute is a part of the system.
- Skills and expertise: At maturity level 1, there is no identification of skills and training requirements. At maturity level 5, there is continual improvement of skills, knowledge sharing, and industry's best practices. The soft skills will contribute to synergy and technical skills are requirement of system.
- Responsibility and accountability: At maturity level 1, responsibility is not defined. At maturity level 5, acceptance of responsibilities is cascaded down throughout the organisation. This attribute is a part of synergy.
- Goal setting and measurement: At maturity level 1, there are no goals and no measurement system. At maturity level 5, there is integrated performance system with individual performance and process performance. This is a part of strategy.

We can determine the meeting process maturity with the above criteria. We will also find the pain points of meetings in the organisation and analyse how process will address the pain points. We will prioritise goals addressing important and high-impact pain points. Goals are set using SMART (specific, measurable, attainable, realistic, and timely) definition (refer outcome frame in Section 6.7).

10.2 Updating Skills or Sharpen the Saw

Business is a dynamic environment where there is a constant change and we experience uncertainty. This gives a challenge of adapting changes and learning new things. Meetings are no exception. New tools and techniques will also be applicable to the meeting environment. This evolves new ways for meetings. Meeting participants should set aside time to update themselves on new concepts, tools, and processes related to meetings. They should attend required trainings.

Meetings use people as resources. Thus, the production capacity of a meeting is dependent on the capacity of participants. Meeting outcomes are the production, and people are production capacity. The production capacity will increase with training and skill development.

Stephen Covey has used the concept production and production capacity with Aesop's fable of golden goose. We can also apply this concept to the meetings. If people are goose and meetings are golden eggs, then organisations may focus only on golden eggs (meetings) and kill the goose (people frustration) and land in problems.

The right approach is to set aside time to develop skills (i.e. sharpening the saw) and use those skills in the meeting to make them efficient, effective, and energetic.

10.3 Balanced Scorecard

Balanced scorecard (BSC) is a useful tool to develop a strategy to improve the process, function, or business. We can apply balanced scorecard to the meetings. Organisations can consider simple strategy on meetings.

Train the staff on the meeting → The meeting process is run efficiently, effectively, and energetically → Satisfied meeting participants → Improved financial result

Four parameters of balanced scorecard will have the following objectives:

- Financial: To maximise utilisation of meetings for value-added activities and minimise meeting costs under overheads.
- Customer: To maximise satisfaction or positive experience of the meeting participants.
- Process: To optimise efficiency, effectiveness, and energy of the meeting process.
- Learning and growth: To develop the skills required for the meeting through trainings and practising in meetings.

Executives or meeting participants need to have certain skills for the meeting. The meeting participants can attend the trainings and practise skills in meetings. The trainings can be listed as follows:

- Communication skills training: This is about verbal and written communication, listening skills, and so on.
- Training for facilitator: This can be generic or specific like six thinking hats.
- Training for coach: Managers need to take this role in one-to-one meeting. Training in coaching is useful.
- Training for problem solving: As discussed in Chapter 7, training on problem-solving tools and techniques is useful.
- NLP trainings: NLP practitioner training course and NLP master practitioner course are available at ANLP to get in-depth knowledge. NLP trainers can provide customised training.
- Negotiation training: This is useful for sales and procurement people.
- Sales training: This is to learn sales process and related skills.
- Leadership trainings: This will cover leadership skills like team building, goal setting, feedback, and so on.

Balanced scorecard sets measurements for each category. The measurement can be the outcome indicators (e.g. number of decisions made and number of action items) or process indicators (e.g. rating for meeting efficiency and rating for meeting effectiveness). The meeting feedback ratings will be one of the important data source, giving various measures or indicators.

- Financial: Meeting cost can be computed using the time spent and hourly rates. We can classify meetings as administrative meetings (part of overheads), meetings related to maintenance (efforts to keep running the systems or fixing the problems), and meetings for value-added activities (efforts leading to revenue generation). We can monitor the costs with reference to these three meeting types. Organisations will focus that maximum meeting time is for value addition and minimal for administrative work. Meeting cost has been discussed in detail in Chapter 2 (Section 2.3). We can get the meeting cost and where it is applicable, we can compute the revenue. For balanced scorecard, the indicator should be easy to compute or else gathering of data will become a tedious activity.

- Customer: Meeting customer and service provider is the same, that is, the meeting participants. Ratings during meeting evaluation can be used for customer satisfaction, especially
  - Synergy experienced
  - Energy experienced
  - Role takers' performance
- Process: Effectiveness and efficiency are important; hence, ratings during meeting feedback on both are useful. The action items completed as planned will also depend on efficiency and effectiveness.
- Learning and growth: The percentage of trained staff can indicate the assurance of conducting meetings successfully. Another training indicator can check trainings planned versus actual training.

The generic strategy map is shown in Figure 10.1.

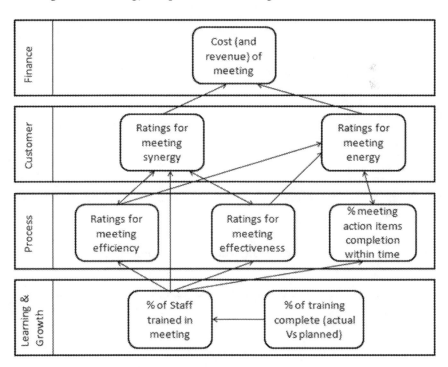

Figure 10.1: Strategy map using balanced scorecard.

The four indicators form the strategy map because the indicators will have an impact on each other.

Further, each department can add their department-specific indicators. Sales department will have meetings with the customers. In case of expensive items, there may be several meetings before customers' decision to buy (or reject). Sales department can have additional indicators in their balanced scorecard. Similarly, the project team will have additional indicators linked to the project management.

10.4   In Summary

Business will remain competitive when it keeps pace with improvements. Balanced scorecard (BSC) is a holistic approach for measuring four major areas—finance, customer, process, and learning and growth of human resources. We can apply balanced scorecard to the meeting with required customisation for department and deliver high performance.

In case of a system, we looked at the tools like maturity assessment and balanced scorecard.

Our strategy is to use balanced scorecard for balanced approach.

10.5   Afterthought

After going through this chapter, you will have thoughts about the discussion in this chapter. Our theme is to build the systems, strategies and synergies for the meetings. With due respect to your model of the world, please jot down your thoughts on systems, strategies and synergies.

- What are the systems needed for a meeting?

_____

_____

_____

• What are the strategies required for a meeting?

_____

_____

_____

• How are the synergies built for a meeting?

_____

_____

_____

APPENDICES

Appendix A. NLP Communication Model

NLP Communication model is studied in detail in NLP course. Here is a brief description.

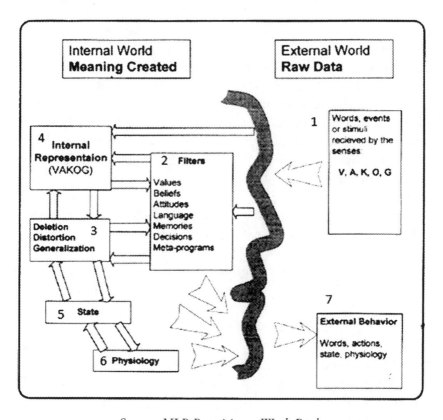

Source: NLP Practitioner Work Book.

1. External Stimulus: Acronym VAKOG is based on our five senses:
   (a) Vision—what we see
   (b) Auditory—what we hear or listen
   (c) Kinaesthetic—what we feel
   (d) Olfactory—what we smell
   (e) Gustatory—what we taste

2. Filters: The information goes through filters like values and beliefs (Chapter 2), meta programmes, and so on. This will impact on information.

3. Deletion, Distortion, and Generalisation: These three filters impact the inputs. Deletion happens as we pay attention to the inputs selectively. Distortion happens when we modify those inputs. Generalisation happens when we put the information under certain category or classification. For example, a purchase manager asked purchase officer, 'What is the status of purchase order number N to the vendor ABC?'

   Purchase officer answered, 'I reminded ABC two days back; delivery may be delayed by two to three days.' The director asked the same question to the purchase manager.

   The purchase manager answered, 'As usual, ABC will delay by a week.' The purchase manager deleted the information about the reminder and distorted the number of days for the delay, and 'as usual' indicates generalisation.

4. Internal Representation: This is an experience stored in our memory. It is in the form of VAKOG, which means all five senses. For example, someone is having a playful Pomeranian dog as a pet. Someone had a dog bite and had to take painful injections. When we say dog, both will have different internal representation because of their experience. Hence, we say everyone is unique and everyone has unique model of the world.

5. State: State of mind means mood or feelings.

6. Physiology: We agree that body and mind are connected. Richard Bandler says body and mind are connected through language or self-talk. Our body speaks same language as our thoughts or feelings, and vice versa is also true. Adopt a physiology of happy state; you will find it difficult to think of a sad state.

7. External Behaviour: The behaviour observed by other persons.

Appendix B. NLP Presuppositions

1. Everyone has a unique model of the world.
2. Respect other person's model of the world.
3. People are map makers.
4. People's map are made of pictures, sounds, feelings, smells, and tastes (VAKOG—visual, auditory, kinaesthetic, olfactory, and gustatory).
5. People respond to their maps of reality, not to reality.
6. The map is not the territory.
7. If you change your map, you will change your emotional state.
8. Behind every behaviour, there is a positive intention.
9. People are not their behaviours.
10. The meaning of behaviour is dependent on the context it is exhibited in.
11. All behaviour has positive intention.
12. The most important thing about a person is that person's behaviour.
13. Every behaviour is useful in some context.
14. The positive worth of an individual is held constant, while the value and appropriateness of internal and/or external behaviour is questioned.
15. A person with the most flexibility in his or her behaviours will have greater influence over others.
16. Choice is better than no choice.
17. People always make the best choices available to them.
18. All procedures should be designed to create choice and promote wholeness.
19. Everyone is doing the best they can with the resources they have available.
20. There are no un-resourceful people but only un-resourceful states.
21. Everyone is in charge of their mind and, therefore, their results.
22. People work perfectly to produce the results they are getting.
23. If one person can do something, anyone can learn to do it.
24. People already have all the resources they need to achieve their desired outcomes.
25. There is no such thing as failure but only feedback.
26. Experience has a structure.

27. If what you are doing is not working, do something else.
28. Positive change always comes from adding resources.
29. The mind and body are parts of the same system and affect each other.
30. The most flexible element in any system can control the system.
31. The meaning of communication is the response you get.
32. Resistance in a client (other person) is lack of rapport.
33. The quality of our lives is determined by the quality of our communication.
34. There is no substitute for clean, open sensory channels.

Appendix C. 7 Habits of Highly Effective People

Stephen Covey's book *The 7 Habits of Highly Effective People* is a holistic integrated guide on effectiveness. When an executive thinks about effectiveness in any area, the points in this book are taken into account. For example, software development organisations or IT departments can use personal software processes and team software processes, which has a base from this book. Meetings have strong connection with this book, and the following points throws light:

- *Be proactive*: Chapter 2 suggests to be proactive in defining the purpose of the meeting and use positive language of a proactive person.
- *Begin with the end in mind*: Chapter 4 is about the preparation for the meeting. Meeting preparation is to be done with this habit in mind. Chapter 6 is about action items. Action items also need this habit.
- *Put first things first*: Chapter 2 discusses that more meetings should be 'important and not urgent' than emergency meetings (important and urgent) or trivial meetings (not important and urgent/not urgent).
- *Think win/win*: Chapters 5 and 7 highlight this habit to achieve solution, satisfying all the parties.
- *Seek first to understand, then to be understood*: Chapter 5 highlights that active listening can happen if we use this habit during the meeting.
- *Synergise*: Chapters 3 and 5 highlight the synergy in the meeting that will deliver high outputs.
- *Sharpen the saw*: Chapter 10 highlights that the meeting participants need trainings in skills to be developed for the meeting.

We consider this book as an excellent book; however, we raise certain barriers when we think about practising it. The intention of mapping seven habits to the meetings is to practise them during the meeting. Meeting process with seven habits is shown in the following figure.

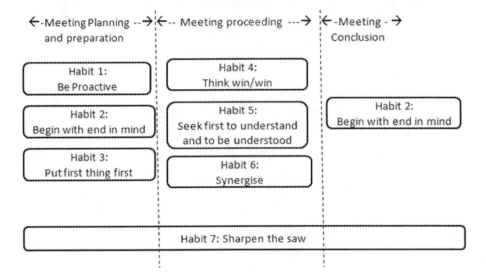

Appendix D. Six Thinking Hats

Edward de Bono invented the concept of six thinking hats method. It is rated as the most important change in human thinking. The thinking productivity increases by five times or nearly 400 per cent. More can be learned by reading books on six thinking hats or by attending training programmes on six thinking hats.

Six thinking hats can be explained in short as follows:

- **White Hat:**
  With white hat, you focus on the data, information, and learning from it. Find out the gaps in your knowledge and either fill them or take an account of them.

- **Yellow Hat:**
  The yellow hat helps you to think positively. Consider optimistic view and see all the benefits of the decision and the value in it.

- **Black Hat:**
  Using black hat thinking, look at all the bad points of the decision. Ponder why it might not work. Find out the weak points in a plan. Eliminate them for prevention, alter them for impact reduction, or prepare contingency plans to counter them.

- **Red Hat:**
  Wearing the red hat, you look at emotional part or impact of the problem. This uses intuition or gut reaction. Also analyse how other people will react emotionally.

- **Green Hat:**
  The green hat is for creativity. Develop creative solutions to a problem. Use different creativity tools and give freedom to think.

- **Blue Hat:**
  The blue hat is for process control. The chairperson or the facilitator wears this hat. Blue hat triggers the other hats as per the needs.

Meeting process with six thinking hats is shown in the following figure.

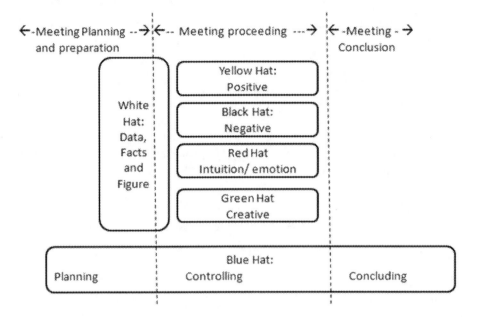

Appendix E. Kepner Tregoe Model

Kepner Tregoe has a popular method for problem solving and decision-making. ITIL (Information Technology Infrastructure Library) developed best practices in the IT service management. It recommends Kepner Tregoe model for problem management process. The detailed model can be studied by reading the book *The Rational Manager* or by attending training programmes. The basic steps in problem solving are listed below:

- Problem Analysis
    - Define problem.
    - Specify problem.
    - Identify differences and changes.
    - Formulate causes.
    - Test causes against the facts.
    - Prove true cause.
- Decision Analysis
    - State the decision.
    - Define and classify objectives.
    - Weigh the objectives.
    - Generate alternatives.
    - Evaluate alternatives.
    - Assess risks.
    - Make decision.
- Potential Problem Analysis
    - Identify potential problem.
    - Identify likely causes.
    - Take preventive action.
    - Plan contingent action and set trigger.
- Supporting Skills for the Above
    - Creative thinking skill
    - Questioning skill
    - Active listening skill

Appendix F. Toastmasters International

Toastmasters International is a non-profit organisation that promotes development of leadership and communication skills. Toastmasters club can be formed within an organisation (called corporate club restricted to the organisation) or within community (called community club which is open to all). Members of the club learn through Toastmasters' meetings. Toastmasters' meetings provide practice on how to plan and conduct a meeting. Education starts with basic communication manual and basic leadership manual. After completion of the basic manuals, there are advanced manuals (Table F.1). For more details, please refer to Toastmasters International's website http://www.toastmasters.org

Table F.1: Advanced manuals and use in meetings

Advanced manual	Learning	Usefulness for meetings
Facilitating discussion	Learn about moderating a panel discussion, facilitating brainstorming meeting, leading a problem-solving discussion, handling challenging people during the discussion, helping a problem-solving group to achieve consensus.	High
Speeches by management	Learn about giving briefings, preparing and presenting technical speeches, motivating a team, giving status report, and speaking to hostile group.	High
The professional speaker	Guidance on preparing and presenting a keynote address, an entertaining speech, a sales training speech, a seminar, and a motivational speech.	High
Persuasive speaking	This covers selling a product, making 'cold calls', preparing a winning proposal, convincing audience on a controversial issue, bringing vision and mission to reality.	High

Interpersonal communication	This covers conversing with ease, negotiating, handling criticism and coach, and expressing dissatisfaction effectively.	High
Technical presentations	Presenting technical information in a way that doesn't bore the audience.	Medium
Public relation	This covers generating a favourable attitude, presenting positive image, radio talk show, persuading audience, and handling crises situation.	Medium
The entertaining speaker	Use of good stories, anecdotes, drama, and humour in speech	Medium
Humorously speaking	Use of humour in the beginning, throughout the speech, and in the end.	Medium
Speaking to inform	This covers informational speech, tailoring to audience, conducting demonstration, presenting report, and speech about abstract subject.	Medium
Speciality speeches	This covers impromptu talk, sales talk, inspirational talk, reading out, and introducing the speaker.	Medium
Storytelling	This covers telling folk tales, personal stories, stories with moral, emotional stories, and historical stories.	Low
Communicating on television	This covers presenting an editorial, being a guest or host for an interview, press conference, and training using TV.	Low
Special occasion speeches	This covers raising toast, speaking in praise, roasting, giving, and accepting award.	Low
Interpretive reading	This covers reading stories, poetry, monodrama, plays, and famous speeches.	Low

Appendix G. Robert's Rulebook

Robert's *Rules of Order* contains rules of order intended to be adopted as a parliamentary authority for use by a deliberative assembly. This is useful for conducting a meeting in democratic way. The rule is, majority rules, but rights of individual, minority, and absent members are protected. The topics covered by this book are the following:

- Organising and conducting business in mass meetings and permanent societies
- Debate, stating, and putting questions, and what motions to use to accomplish certain objects
- How to find if a motion is in order, if it can be debated, amended, or reconsidered, and if it requires a second, or a 2/3 vote, etc.
- Definition and how to find rulings in the manual
- Amendments
- Classification of motions and most of the privileged ones
- Orders of the day, and definite and indefinite postponement
- Laying aside a question temporarily, resuming its consideration, and closing and limiting debate
- The motion to commit, and committees
- Committees (concluded)
- Reconsidering and rescinding a vote
- Some miscellaneous and incidental motions
- Incidental motions (concluded)
- Debate
- Voting
- The officers and the minutes
- Nominations and elections, and miscellaneous
- Rules of an assembly and their amendments

Bibliography

- *NLP Practitioner Work Book*, compiled, written and edited by David J. Lincoln, ANLP India (2012).
- *Master Practitioner of NLP*, compiled, written and edited by David J. Lincoln, ANLP India (2012).
- *NLP Trainers Training*, compiled, edited by David J. Lincoln, ANLP India (2012).
- *NLP for Curious*, David J. Lincoln, ANLP India (2012).
- *NLP at Work: The Difference that Makes the Difference in Business*, Sue Knight, Nicholas Brealey, London (2nd edition, 2002).
- *Modelling with NLP*, Roberts Dilts, Meta Publication, Capitola, CA99333999 (1998).
- *Words That Change Minds: Mastering the Language of Influence*, Shelle Rose Charvet, Success Strategy, Kendall/Hunt Publishing, Dubuque, IA (1997).
- *Live Your Dream: Let Reality Catch-Up*, Rogger Ellerton, Trafford Publishing, Bloomington, IN (2006).
- *Play Magic Golf: How to use self-hypnosis, meditation, Zen, universal laws, qualtun energy and latest psychological and NLP techniques to be better golfer,* Stephen Simpson MX Publishing, London (2010).
- *Countermove: A Guide to the Art of Negotiation*, Ralph Watson, published by Ralph Watson (2009).
- *Seeing Spells Achieving*, Olive Hickmott and Andrew Bendefy, MX Publishing, London (2006).
- *Online Therapy—Reading between the Lines*, Jethro Adlington, MX Publishing, London (2009).
- *Mind with a Heart*, Richard P. McHugh, Gujarat Sahitya Prakash, Anand, India (6th edition, 2009).
- *Awken the Giant Within: How to take the Immediate Control of your Mental, Emotional, Physical and Financial Destiny,* Anthony Robbins, Simon and Schuster Ltd. (1997)
- *Six Thinking Hats*, Edward de Bono, Penguin Books, London (1999).
- *Teaching Yourself to Think*, Edward de Bono, Penguin Books, London (1995).

- *How Successful People Think*, John C. Maxwell, Center Street, New York (2009).
- *The 7 Habits of Highly Effective People*, Stephen Covey, Pocket Book, New York (2004).
- *Laugh & Get Rich: How to Profit from Humor in Any Business*, Rick Segel and Darren LaCroix, Specific House, Kissimmee, FL (7th print, 2009).
- *Brilliant Decision Making*, Robbie Steinhouse, Pearson Education Limited, Upper Saddle River, NJ (2010).
- *Think Like an Entrepreneur*, Robbie Steinhouse and Chris West, Pearson Education Limited, Upper Saddle River, NJ (2008).
- Website: http://www.belbin.com
- *Humor Is No Laughing Matter*, Ross Mackay, Ross Mackey, Aurora, ON (2006).
- *Communication and Leadership Program Manual (for Competent Communicator)*, Toastmasters International Inc., Rancho Santa Margarita, CA (2003).
- *Toastmasters' advanced communication manuals series*, Toastmasters International Inc., Rancho Santa Margarita, CA(2008)
- *Facilitating Group Discussion: Understanding Group Development and Dynamics*, Kathy Takamaya, Brown University, Essay on 'Teaching excellence: towards the best in the academy', Vol. 21, No. 1, 2009-10.
- *Team Players and Teamwork: New Strategy for Developing Successful Collaboration*, Glenn M. Parker, John Wiley & Sons, New York (2008).
- *Improving Group, Organisational or Team Dynamics When Conflict Occurs*, Howard Culbertson, Southern Nazarene University, Bethany, OK (2001). (http://snu.edu)
- Working Globally Aperian Global (http://corp.aperianglobal.com).
- http://www.rulesonline.com (Robert's rulebook).
- *How to Run an Effective Meeting*, by Barry L. Shoop, presentation at IEEE Region 1 Summer Meeting (2003) Schenectady, New York.
- *Launching your career: a Practitioner's guide to Leadership*, Barry L. Shoop, Ph.D. IEEE-USA (2009)
- Conference Centre, Seating style, University of Waterloo (http://www.uwaterloo.ca)
- http://www.ikedaquotes.org
- http://www.wikipedia.org
- http://www.mindtools.com
- COBIT 4.1, IT Governance Institute, USA (2007)

Index

Wish to learn more? Contact

PQR Consulting Services LLP, Pune, India

We conduct training courses—NLP practitioner, meeting magic (combining meeting protocol and NLP), nlp4quality (combining NLP with quality concepts), and customised courses for corporate. We coach executives and professionals.

For more information, visit www.qualitynlpcoach.com or email info@qualitynlpcoach.com